SCANDINAVIAN INFLUENCE ON
SOUTHERN LOWLAND SCOTCH

GEORGE TOBIAS FLOM
SOMETIME FELLOW IN GERMAN,
COLUMBIA UNIVERSITY

SCANDINAVIAN INFLUENCE ON SOUTHERN LOWLAND SCOTCH

A CONTRIBUTION TO THE STUDY OF THE LINGUISTIC RELATIONS OF ENGLISH AND SCANDINAVIAN

BIBLIOBAZAAR

SCANDINAVIAN INFLUENCE ON SOUTHERN LOWLAND SCOTCH

CONTENTS

TO

PROF. WILLIAM H. CARPENTER, PH.D.
PROF. CALVIN THOMAS, A.M.
PROF. THOMAS R. PRICE, LL.D.
OF COLUMBIA UNIVERSITY IN THE CITY OF NEW YORK

IN GRATITUDE

PREFACE.

This work aims primarily at giving a list of Scandinavian loanwords found in Scottish literature. The publications of the Scottish Text Society and Scotch works published by the Early English Text Society have been examined. To these have been added a number of other works to which I had access, principally Middle Scotch. Some words have been taken from works more recent—"Mansie Wauch" by James Moir, "Johnnie Gibb" by William Alexander, Isaiah and The Psalms by P. Hately Waddell— partly to illustrate New Scotch forms, but also because they help to show the dialectal provenience of loanwords. Norse elements in the Northern dialects of Lowland Scotch, those of Caithness and Insular Scotland, are not represented in this work. My list of loanwords is probably far from complete. A few early Scottish texts I have not been able to examine. These as well as the large number of vernacular writings of the last 150 years will have to be examined before anything like completeness can be arrived at.

I have adopted certain tests of form, meaning, and distribution. With regard to the test of the form of a word great care must be exercised. Old Norse and Old Northumbrian have a great many characteristics in common, and some of these are the very ones in which Old Northumbrian differs from West Saxon. It has, consequently, in not a few cases, been difficult to decide whether a word is a loanword or not. Tests that apply in the South prove nothing for the North. Brate rightly regarded *leȝȝkenn* in the Ormulum as a Scandinavian loanword, but in Middle Scotch *laiken* or *laken* would be the form of the word whether Norse or genuine English. Certain well-known tests of form, however, first formulated by Brate, such as *ou* for O. E. *ea*, or the assimilation of certain consonants apply as well to Scotch as to Early Middle English. The distribution of a word in English dialects frequently helps to ascertain its real history, and may become a final test where those of form and meaning leave us in doubt. In the study of Norse or Scandinavian influence on Lowland Scotch the question of Gaelic influence cannot be overlooked. The extent of Norse influence on Celtic in Caithness, Sutherland and the Western Highlands, has never been ascertained, nor the influence of Celtic on Lowland Scotch. A large number of Scandinavian loanwords are common to Gaelic, Irish, and Lowland Scotch. It is possible that some of these have come into Scotch through Gaelic and not directly from Norse. Perhaps *faid*, "a company of hunters," is such a word.

There are no works bearing directly on the subject of Scandinavian elements in Lowland Scotch proper. J. Jakobsen's work, "Det norrøne Sprog på Shetland," has sometimes given me valuable hints. From Brate's well-known work on the Ormulum I have derived a great deal of help. Steenstrup's "Danelag" has been of assistance to me, as also Kluge's "Geschichte der englischen Sprache" in Paul's Grundriss, the latter especially with regard to characteristics of Northern English. Wall's work on "Scandinavian Elements in English Dialects" has been especially helpful because of the excellent list of loanwords given. In many cases, however, my own investigations have led me to different conclusions, principally with regard to certain tests and the dialectal provenience of loanwords. Finally, the excellent editions of Scottish texts published by the S.T.S. and the E.E.T.S. have made the work less difficult than it otherwise would have been. I may mention particularly "The Bruce," Dunbar, and Montgomery, where Scandinavian elements are very prominent.

ABBREVIATIONS REFERRING TO TEXTS INCLUDED IN THIS INVESTIGATION.[1]

K.Q. = The "Kingis Quair" of James I., ed. W.W. Skeat. S.T.S. 1.

Dunbar = Bishop Dunbar's Works, ed. by John Small, R.J.G. Mackay and W. Gregor. S.T.S. 2, 4, 16, 21, 29.

Rolland = "The Court of Venus" by John Rolland, ed. W. Gregor. S.T.S. 3.

Dalr. = Leslie's History of Scotland, translated by Dalrymple, ed. E.G. Cody. S.T.S. 5, 14, 19, 34.

Wallace = Henry the Minstrel's "Wallace," ed. James Moir. S.T.S. 6, 7, 17.

Montg. = Alexander Montgomery's Poems, ed. James Cranstoun. S.T.S. 9, 10, 11.

Gau = "Richt way to the hevinlie Kingdom," by John Gau, ed. A.F. Mitchell. S.T.S. 12.

Winyet = "Certain Tractates," by Ninian Winyet, ed. J.K. Hewison. S.T.S. 15, 52.

Sat. P. = Satirical Poems of the Time of the Reformation, ed. J. Cranstoun. S.T.S. 20, 24, 28, 30.

Buchanan = Vernacular Writings of George Buchanan, ed. P.H. Brown. S.T.S. 26.

Bruce = Barbour's "Bruce," ed. W.W. Skeat. E.E.T.S. Extra Series II, 21, 29.

Lyndsay = Sir David Lyndsay's Works, containing "The Monarchie," "Squire Meldrum," "The Dream," and "Ane Satire of the Three Estates," ed. F. Hall. E.E.T.S. 11, 19, 35, 37.

C.S.= "The Complaynt of Scotland," ed. J.A.H. Murray. E.E.T.S. 17.

L.L.= "Lancelot of the Laik," ed. W.W. Skeat. E.E.T.S. 6.

R.R. = "Ratis Raving" and other Moral and Religious Pieces in Prose and Verse, ed. J. Rawson Lumby. E.E.T.S. 43.

Douglas = The Poetical Works of Gawain Douglas in 4 vols., ed. John Small. Edinburgh. 1874.

Wyntoun = "The Orygynale Cronykil of Scotland," by Andrew of Wyntoun, ed. David McPherson. 2 vols. London. 1795.

R. and L. = "Roswell and Lillian," ed. O. Lengert. Englische Studien 16.

Gol. and Gaw. = "Golagros and Gawain," ed. Moritz Trautmann. Anglia II.

Scott = The Poems of Alexander Scott, ed. Andrew Laing. Edinburgh. 1821.

Philotus = "Philotus, A Comedy imprinted at Edinburgh by Robert Charters, 1603." Published by the Bannatyne Club. Edinburgh. 1835.

Anc. Pro. = Collection of Ancient Scottish Prophecies in Alliterative Verse, 1603. Published by the Bannatyne Club. 1833.

Poet. Rem. = The Poetical Remains of Some of the Scottish Kings, containing "Peblis to the Play," "Christ's Kirk on the Green," "The Gaberlunzie Man," and "Ane Ballad of Good Council," ed. George Chalmers. London. 1824.

Sco. Poems = Scottish Poems in 3 vols. containing "The Tales of the Priests of Peblis," "Ballads" (1508), Holland's "Howlate," "The Bloody Sark" of Robert Henrison, and "Sir Gawain and Sir Galaron" of Galloway. London. 1792.

A.P.B.S. = Ancient Popular Ballads and Songs, ed. Robert Jamieson. Edinburgh. 1806.

Fergusson = The Works of Robert Fergusson, ed. David Irving. Greenock. 1810.

Irving = History of Scottish Poetry, containing a number of extracts, ed. David Irving. Edinburgh. 1874.

Scotticisms = Scotticisms Corrected. London. 1855.

Ramsay = The Poems of Allan Ramsay, in 2 vols. Printed by A. Strahan for T. Cadwell and W. Davies. London. 1800.

Burns = The Works of Robert Burns, ed. Dr. Adolphus Wagner. Leipzig. 1835.

Isaiah = Isaiah, frae Hebrew intil Scottis, by P. Hately Waddell. Edinburgh and Glasgow. 1879.

Psalms = The Psalms, frae Hebrew intil Scottis, by P. Hately Waddell. Edinburgh and Glasgow. 1891.

M.W. = "Mansie Wauch," by D.M. Moir. Edinburgh. 1898. Centenary Edition.

J.G. = "Johnnie Gibb of Gushetneuk," by William Alexander (1871). Edinburgh. 1897.

ABBREVIATIONS REFERRING TO GRAMMARS, GLOSSARIES, DICTIONARIES, AND THE LIKE

Aasen = Norsk Ordbog, af Ivar Aasen. Christiania. 1873. Generally referred to as Norse.

B-T. = The Bosworth-Toller Anglo-Saxon Dictionary. Referred to generally as Old English.

B-S. = Bradley's Stratmann's Middle English Dictionary. References to Middle English forms are to B-S., unless otherwise specified.

Brate = "Nordische Lehnwörter im Ormulum." Paul und Braunes Beiträge, X. 1885.

Brem. W. = Bremisch-Niedersächsisches Wörterbuch. Bremen. 1767.

Bouterwek = Die vier Evangelien in alt-nordhumbrischer Sprache. Karl Bouterwek. Gütersloh. 1857.

Cl. and V. = Cleasby and Vigfusson's Icelandic-English Dictionary. Oxford. 1874. Old Norse words have been taken largely from Cl. and V.

Cook = A Glossary of the Old Northumbrian Gospels. A.S. Cook. Halle. 1894.

Craigie = Oldnordiske Ord i de gæliske Sprog. W.A. Craigie, in Arkiv for nordisk Filologie X. pp. 149ff.

Curtis = An Investigation of the Rimes and Phonology of the Middle Scotch Romance "Clariodus," by F.J. Curtis, in Anglia XVI and XVII.

Dickinson = A Glossary of the Words and Phrases of Cumberland. William Dickinson. Whitehaven and London. 1859.

D.S.C.S. = The Dialect of the Southern Counties of Scotland, by J.A.H. Murray. London. 1873.

Egge = Norse words in the Anglo-Saxon Chronicle. Albert Egge. Pullman, Washington. 1898.

E.D.D. = The English Dialect Dictionary, A to C, ed. Joseph Wright. Oxford. 1898.

Ellis = On Early English Pronunciation. Vol. 5, by Alexander J. Ellis. Early English Text Society, Extra Series 56.

Fritzner = Ordbog over det gamle norske Sprog. Johan Fritzner. Christiania. 1886-1896.

Gibson = The Folkspeech of Cumberland, by A.C. Gibson. London. 1873.

Haldorson = Lexicon Islandico-Latino-Danicum, Biornonis Haldorsonii. Havniae. 1814.

Jakobsen = Det norrøne Sprog på Shetland, by J. Jakobsen. Köbenhavn. 1897. Shetland dialect forms are generally taken from this work.

Jamieson = Jamieson's Dictionary of the Scottish Language.

Jellinghaus = Angelsächsisch-Neuenglische Wörter, die nicht niederdeutsch sind, by H. Jellinghaus, in Anglia XX. Pp. 46-466.

Kalkar = Ordbog til det ældre danske Sprog. Otto Kalkar. Köbenhavn. 1881-1892.

Lindelöf = Glossar zur altnordhumbrischen Evanglienübersetzung in der Rushworth-Handschrift (in Acta Societatis Scientiarum Fennicae Tome XXII., No. 5), von Uno Lindelöf. Helsingfors. 1897.

Kluge P. G.^{2} I. = Kluge's "Geschichte der englischen Sprache," in Paul's Grundriss, 2 Auflage, I Band.

Kluge and Lutz = English Etymology, by F. Kluge and F. Lutz. Strassburg. 1898.

Koolman = Wörterbuch der ostfriesischen Sprache. J. ten Doornkaat Koolman. Norden. 1879-1884. Sometimes cited as Low German.

Luik = Untersuchungen zur englischen Lautgeschichte. Strassburg. 1896.

Molbech = Dansk Ordbog. C. Molbech. Kjöbenhavn. 1859. Referred to generally as Danish.

N.E.D. = The New English Dictionary, A to Frankish, ed. J.A.H. Murray.

Noreen P. G.² I. = Noreen's "Geschichte der nordischen Sprachen," in Paul's Grundriss, 2 Auflage, 1 Band.

Kluge = Etymologisches Wörterbuch der deutschen Sprache. Friedrich Kluge. Strassburg. 1894.

Richthofen (or O. F.) = Altfriesisches Wörterbuch, von Karl Freiherrn von Richthofen. Göttingen. 1840.

Rietz (or Sw. dial.) = Svenskt Dialekt-Lexikon. J.E. Rietz. Malmö. 1867.

Ross = Norsk Ordbog. Tillæg til Ivar Aasen's Ordbog. Hans Ross. Christiania. 1895.

Schiller und Lübben = Mittelniederdeutsches Wörterbuch. Bremen. 1875-1880. Cited as M.L.G.

Schlyter = Glossarium til Skånelagen (Sveriges Gamle Lagar IX.). C.J. Schlyter. Lund. 1859.

O.S. = Old Saxon. Schmellers Glossarium Saxonicum e Poemate Heliand. Tübingae. 1840.

Sievers = Altenglische Grammatik. Eduard Sievers. 3 Auflage. 1898.

Skeat = Etymological Dictionary of the English Language. Oxford. 1882; and Concise Etymological Dictionary. Oxford. 1897.

Skeat's list = A List of English Words, the Etymology of which is illustrated by Comparison with Icelandic. W.W. Skeat. Oxford. 1876.

Steenstrup = Danelag (Vol. IV. of "Normannerne"). J.C.H.R. Steenstrup. Kjöbenhavn. 1882.

Sweet = Student's Anglo-Saxon Dictionary. Henry Sweet. Oxford. 1897.

Söderwall = Ordbok öfver svenska Medeltids Språket, A to L. K.F. Söderwall. Lund. 1884-1890.

Thorkelson = Supplement til islandske Ordböger. Jon Thorkelson. Reykjavik. 1876-1897.

Wall = "Scandinavian Elements in the English Dialects," by Arnold Wall. Anglia XX.

Worsaae = Minder om de Danske og Normændene i England, Skotland, og Irland, af J.J.A. Worsaae. Kjöbenhavn. 1851.

ABBREVIATIONS REFERRING TO LANGUAGES, GRAMMATICAL TERMS, ETC.

adj. = adjective.
adv. = adverb.
cp. = compare.
conj. = conjunction.
Cu. = Cumbrian, Cumberland.
Dan. = New or Modern Danish.
dem. pr. = demonstrative pronoun.
deriv. = derivative.
dial. = dialect, dialectal.
diall. = dialects.
E. Norse = East Norse.
Eng. = English, standard speech.
Far. = Faroese.
Fr. = French.
Gael. = Gaelic.
Germ. = German.
Gmc. = Germanic.
Goth. = Gothic.
id. = the same.
inf. = infinitive.
Ir. = Irish.
L. G. = Low German.
M. Dan. = Middle Danish.
M. Du. = Middle Dutch.

M. E. = Middle English.

M. H. G. = Middle High German.

M. L. G. = Middle Low German.

M. Sco. = Middle Scotch.

M. Sw. = Middle Swedish.

Norse = New or Modern Norse.

N. Sco. = Modern Scotch dialects.

O. Dan. = Old Danish.

O. E. = Old English.

O. F. = Old Frisian.

O. Fr. = Old French.

O. Ic. = Old Icelandic.

O. N. = Old Norse.

O. Nh. = Old Northern.

O. Nhb. = Old Northumbrian.

O. S. = Old Saxon.

O. Sw. = Old Swedish.

p. = page; pp. = pages.

p. p. = past participle.

pr. p. = present participle.

pret. = preterite.

pron. = pronounced.

prep. = preposition.

pl. = plural.

q.v. = quod vide.

Scand. = Scandinavian.

Sco. = Scotch.

S. S. = Southern Scotland.

sb. = substantive.

Sw. = Swedish.

vb. = verb.

W. Norse = West Norse.

W. Scand. = West Scandinavian.

W. S. = West Saxon.

> = developed into.

< = derived from.

E.D.S. = English Dialect Society.

E.E.T.S. = Early English Text Society.

S.T.S. = Scottish Text Society.

PART I.

INTRODUCTION.

1. General Remarks.

Worsaae's list of 1400 place-names in England gives us an idea of the extent, as well as the distribution of Scandinavian settlements in the 9th and 10th centuries. How long Scandinavian was spoken in England we do not know, but it is probable that it began to merge into English at an early date. The result was a language largely mixed with Norse and Danish elements. These are especially prominent in the M. E. works "Ormulum," "Cursor Mundi," and "Havelok." We have historical records of the Danes in Central and Eastern England. We have no such records of Scandinavian settlements in Northwestern England, but that they took place on an extensive scale 300 place-names in Cumberland and Westmoreland prove. In Southern Scotland, there are only about 100 Scandinavian place-names, which would indicate that such settlements here were on a far smaller scale than in Yorkshire, Lincolnshire, or Cumberland—which inference, however, the large number of Scandinavian elements in Early Scotch seems to disprove. I have attempted to ascertain how extensive these elements are in the literature of Scotland. It is possible that the settlements were more numerous than place-names indicate, that they took place at a later date, for instance, than those in Central England. Brate showed that the general character of Scandinavian loanwords in the Ormulum is East Scandinavian. Wall concludes that it is not possible to determine the exact source of the loanwords in modern English dialects because "the dialect spoken by the Norsemen and the Danes at the time of settlement had not become sufficiently differentiated to leave any distinctive trace in the loanwords borrowed from them, or (that) neither race preponderated in any district so far as to leave any distinctive mark upon the dialect of the English peasantry." It is true that the general character of the language of the two races was at the time very much the same, but some very definite dialectal differentiations had already taken place, and I believe the dialectal provenience of a very large number of the loanwords can be determined. Furthermore, the distribution of certain place-names indicates that certain parts were settled more especially by Danes, others by Norsemen. The larger number of loanwords in Wall's "List A" seem to me to be Danish. My own list of loanwords bears a distinctively Norse stamp, as I shall show in Part III. of this work. This we should also expect, judging from the general character of Scandinavian place-names in Southern Scotland.

2. Place-Names and Settlements in Northwestern England.

Cumberland and Westmoreland, together covering an area equal to about two-thirds that of Yorkshire, have 300 Scandinavian place-names. Yorkshire has 407 according to Worsaae's table. The character of these names in Cumberland and Westmoreland is different from that of those in the rest of England. It seems that these counties were settled predominantly by Norsemen and also perhaps at a later date than that which we accept for the settlements in York and Lincolnshire. We know that as early as 795 Norse vikings began their visits to Ireland; that they settled and occupied the Western Isles about that time; that in 825 the Faroes were first colonized by Norsemen, partly from the Isles. After 870 Iceland was settled by Norsemen from Norway, but in part also from the Western Isles and Ireland. The 'Austmen' in Ireland, especially Dublin, seem frequently to have visited the opposite shore. It seems probable that

24

Northwestern England was settled chiefly by Norsemen from Ireland, Man, and the Isles on the west. It is not likely that any settlements took place before 900. It seems more probable that they belong rather to the second quarter of the 10th Century or even later, when the Irish began successfully to assert themselves against the Norse kings in Dublin and Waterford. Perhaps some may have taken place even as late as the end of the 10th Century.

3. Scandinavian Settlements in Southern Scotland.

In Southern Scotland, Dumfriesshire, Eastern Kircudbright and Western Roxburgh seem to have formed the center of Scandinavian settlements; so, at any rate, the larger number of place-names would indicate. The dialect spoken here is in many respects very similar to that of Northwestern England, D. 31 in Ellis, and the general character of the place-names is the same. These are, however, far fewer than in Northwestern England. Worsaae gives a list of about 30. This list is not exhaustive. From additional sources, rather incomplete, I have been able to add about 80 more Scandinavian place-names that occur in Southern Scotland, most of them of the same general character as those in Northwestern England. Among them: Applegarth, Cogarth, Auldgirth, Hartsgarth, Dalsgairth, Tundergarth, Stonegarthside, Helbeck, Thornythwaite, Twathwaite, Robiethwaite, Murraythwaite, Lockerby, Alby, Denbie, Middlebie, Dunnabie, Wysebie, Perceby, Newby, Milby, Warmanbie, Sorbie, Canoby, Begbie, Sterby, Crosby, Bushby, Magby, Pockby, Humbie, Begbie, Dinlaybyre, Maybole, Carnbo, Gateside, Glenholm, Broomholm, Twynholm, Yetholm, Smailholm, Langholm, Cogar, Prestwick, Fenwick, Howgate, Bowland, Arbigland, Berwick, Southwick, Corstorphine, Rowantree, Eggerness, Southerness, Boness, etc. There are in all about 110 such place-names, with a number of others that may be either English or Scandinavian. The number of Scandinavian elements in Southern Scotch is, however, very great and indicates larger settlements than can be inferred from place-names alone. In the case of early settlements these will generally represent fairly well the extent of settlement. But where they have taken place comparatively late, or where they have been of a more peaceful nature, the number of new names of places that result from them may not at all indicate their extent. The Scandinavians that settled in Southern Scotland probably at no time exceeded in number the native population. The place-names would then for the most part remain unchanged. The loanwords found in Southern Scotch and the names of places resemble those of Northwestern England. The same Northern race that located in Cumberland and Westmoreland also located in Scotland. It is probable, as Worsaae believed, that it is a second migration, chiefly from Cumberland. Dumfriesshire, at any rate, may have been settled in this way. The settlers of Kircudbright and Wigtown were probably largely from the Isles on the west. Other independent settlements were made in Lothian and the region about the Forth. That these are all later than those of Cumberland and Westmoreland is probable. According to what has been said above, the settlements in Dumfries, which seem to have been the earliest, could not have taken place before about the second quarter of the 10th Century, and probably were made later. The other settlements in Southern Scotland may extend even into the 11th Century. The name Dingwall (O. N. *Ðingvöllr*) in Dumfries, the place where the laws were announced annually, indicates a rather extensive settlement in Dumfries, and the dialect of Dumfries is also characterized by a larger number of Scandinavian elements than the rest of the Southern counties.

4. Settlements in England, Norse or Danish? The Place-Name Test.

That the Danes were more numerous than the Norsemen in Central and Eastern England from Northumberland down to the Thames there can be no doubt. The distinctive Norse names *fell*, *tarn* and *force* do not occur at all, while *thorpe* and *toft*, which are as distinctively Danish, are confined almost exclusively to this section. In Northumberland, Durham, Cumberland, Westmoreland and Lancashire *thorpe* is comparatively rare, while *toft* is not found at all. On the other hand, *fell, dale, force, haugh,* and *tarn* (O. N. *fjall, dalr, foss* and *fors, haugr, tjörn*) occur in large numbers in Northwestern England. *Beck* may be either Danish or Norse, occurs, however, chiefly in the North. *Thwaite* Worsaae regarded as Danish "because it occurs generally along with the Danish *by*." We find, however, that this is not exactly the case. In Lincolnshire there are 212 *by's*, in Leicestershire 66, in Northampton 26; *thwaite* does not occur at all. In Yorkshire there are 167 names in *by* and only 8 in *thwaite*, and 6 of these are in West Riding. It is only in Cumberland and Westmoreland that the proportions are nearly the same, but on *by* see below § 5. *Tveit* is far more common in Norway than *tved* in Denmark. The form of the word in place-names in England is, furthermore, more Norse than Danish. In the earliest Scandinavian settlements in England, those of Lincolnshire, for instance, *thwaite* might be Danish if it occurred, for monophthongation of *æi* to *e* did not take place in Danish before about the end of the 9th Century; by about 900 this was complete (see § 6). The Scandinavian settlements in Northwestern England, however, did not take place so early, consequently if these names were Danish and not Norse we should expect to find *thwet*, or *thweet* (*tweet*), in place of *thwaite*. It is then to be regarded as Norse and not Danish. *Thwaite* occurs almost exclusively in Northwestern England—43 times in Cumberland as against 3 in the rest of England south of Yorkshire. *Garth* (O. N. *garðr*, O. Dan. *gardh*, later *gaard*), occurs very often in Cumberland. *With, ness, holm, land,* and *how*, do not occur very often. *How* reminds one of the Jutish *höw* in Modern Danish dialect. The rest of these may be either Danish or Norse. In Yorkshire we find a mixed condition of affairs. East Riding, as we should expect, has predominantly Danish names. *Thorpe*, which occurs 63 times in Lincolnshire, is found 48 times in East Riding. *Fell, tarn* and *haugh* do not occur. *Force* is found twice, and *thwaite* once. *Dale*, however, occurs 12 times. West Riding was probably settled by Danes from the East and by Norsemen from the West. *Thorpe* occurs 29 times, *with* 8, *toft* 2, *beck* 4, *fell* 15, *thwaite* 6, *dale* 12, and *tarn* 2. In North Riding *thorpe* occurs 18 times. *Force*, *fell*, and *tarn* together 12. The large number of names in *dale* in North Riding is rather striking (40 in all), as compared with 52 for Westmoreland and Cumberland. While *dale* is predominantly Norse, it may perfectly well be Danish, and it is not rare in Denmark. Furthermore, the greater number of *dales* in Norway as compared with Denmark is largely accounted for by the nature of the country. No conclusions can be drawn from names in *force* in Yorkshire, Cumberland and Westmoreland, as it is of too infrequent occurrence. *Fell* occurs 22 times in York, as against 57 in Cumberland and Westmoreland (42 in Westmoreland alone), but in York occurs predominantly in West Riding, where everything points to a mixed settlement. The distribution of *tarn* is interesting. *Tarn* is as distinctively Norse as *thorpe* is Danish. It occurs 24 times in Cumberland and Westmoreland, 3 in North Riding, and is not found at all south of Westmoreland and York.

5. *By* in Place-Names. Conclusions as to this Test.

By has been regarded as a sign of Danish settlement for the following reasons: (1) O. N. *bör* would have given *bo*. The O. Dan. form *býr* becomes *by*. (2) *By* is peculiar to Denmark, rare in Norway. (3) *Bö* or *bo* is the form found in Insular Scotland, in the Faroes and other Norse settlements. First, the form *býr* is not exclusively O. Dan. It occurs several times in Old Norse sagas in the form *býr* and *bÿ*—in "Flateyarbók," III., 290, in "Fagrskinna" 41, several times in the "Heimskringla," as well as elsewhere. Again, J. Vibe (see Nordisk Tidskrift, 1884, 535, and Norsk Historisk Tidskrift, 2 Række, 5 Bind), has shown that *by* is not peculiar to Denmark and rare in Norway. It occurs 600-700 times in Denmark and Skåne, and 450 times in Norway. Finally, *by* is often found in Norse settlements in Scotland and elsewhere—in Iceland, Shetland, Orkney, Man, and in the Western Isles. In fact, *by* seems to be the more common form outside of Iceland. All we can say then is that *by* is more Danish than Norse, but may also be Norse. Where names in *by* are numerous it indicates that the settlements are rather Danish, but they may also be Norse. We have, then, the following results: Predominantly Danish settlements: Essex, Bedford, Buckingham, Suffolk, Norfolk, Northampton, Leicester, Rutland, Lincoln, Nottingham, Derby, East Riding. Mixed Norse and Danish settlements: North Riding, West Riding, Durham, part of Cheshire, and Southern Lancashire. Norse settlements: Cumberland, Westmoreland, North Lancashire, part of Cheshire, and parts of Northumberland. The number of Scandinavian place-names in Northumberland is not large, only 22 in Worsaae's list. North of the Cheviot Hills the names are again predominantly Norse.

6. Characteristics of Old Northern, or Old Scandinavian. Early Dialectal Differentiations.

On the characteristics of primitive Northern and the changes that had taken place in the language before the Viking period, see Noreen, P. G.[2] I, 521-526. On pp. 523-526 are summarized the characteristics of General Northern. Until 800 the Northern tongue was unitary throughout the Scandinavian North. In the Viking age dialectal differentiations began to appear, especially in O. Dan. These are as follows (from Noreen):

About 800, older *hr* > *r* in Denmark.
Soon after 800, older diphthongs became simplified in Denmark, *e.g.*,
   au > *u* cp. O. Ic. *þau*, O. Gutnic *þaun* = O. Dan. *þusi* pronounced *þøsi*.
   ai, ei > *i* cp. O. Ic. *stein*, O. N. *stæin*, O. Gtnc. *stain* = O. Dan. *stin*.
   io, iau > *u* cp. O. N., O. Ic. *briote*, O. Gtnc. *briauti* = O. Dan. *biruti*.
Before 1000, *ę* > *æ* cp. O. N., O. Ic. *sér* = O. Dan. *sær* (written *sar*).
About 1,000, appears in O. Sw.—O. Dan. an excrescent *d* between *nn* and *r*, e.g., *mantr*, pronounced *mandr* (see Noreen, p. 526).

7. Old Norse and Old Danish.

Not until the year 1,000, or the beginning of the 11th Century, do dialectal differentiations seem to be fully developed. O. N., which in general preserves best the characteristics of the old Northern speech, undergoes at this time a few changes that differentiate Dan. and Norse still more. O. Sw. remains throughout closer to O. Dan. The two together are therefore called East Scandinavian. Old Icelandic, that is, Norse on Icelandic soil, develops its own forms, remaining, however, in the main very similar to O. N. These two are then called West Scandinavian. The following are some of the chief differences between West and East Scandinavian at the time (from Noreen, P. G.² I, 527):

1. *I—(R)* and *U—Umlaut* in W. S.
Absence of it in E. S., e.g.,

W. S. *hældr*   E. S. *halder.*
 3 sg. pres. of *halda*, "to hold."
W. S. *i gær*, "yesterday," E. S. *i gar.*
W. S. *lǫnd*, pl. "land," E. S. *land.*

2. Development of *i, e, y* into a consonantal *i* in diphthongs in
    W. S., not so in E. S., e.g.,

W. S. *siá*, "to see,"   E. S. *sça.*
W. S. *fiánde*, "enemy," E. S. *fiande.*
W. S. *biár*, "of a village," E. S. *býar.*

3. Assimilation of *mp, nk, nt*, respectively, to *pp, kk, tt* in W. S.,
    retention of them in E. S., e.g.,

W. S. *kroppen*, "crippled," E. S. *krumpin.*
W. S. *ækkia*, "widow,"   E. S. *ankia.*

W. S. *batt*, "bound,"   E. S. *binda.*
  pret. of *binda,*

4. The Medio-passive:

W. S. *sk*, e.g., *kallask*,   E. S. *s, kallas.*

5. Pronominal forms:

W. S. *ek, vér (mér), ér (þer), sem*,   E. S. *iak, vîr, îr, sum.*

8. Remarks.

Assimilation of *mp* to *pp* and *nk* to *kk* appears also quite early in Danish and Swedish, e.g., *kap* (*kapp*) and *drocken* (see Kalkar), *kapp* and *drokken* (Sw.). *U—Umlaut* seems to be more limited in O. N. than in O. Ic. O. Ic. *hl, hn, hr* initially appear early as simple *l, n, r* in O. N. (see Noreen 528), e.g., O. Ic. *hlaupa*, O. N. *loupa*; O. Ic. *hniga*, O. N. *niga*; O. Ic. *hringr*, O. N. *ringr*; O. Ic. *fn* appears in O. N. as *bn* or *mn*, e.g., O. Ic. *nafn*, O. N. *namn* (N. Norse *navn, nabn, namn*). Initial *hv*, which was a heavy guttural spirant, became *kv* in Western Norway, *kv* and *khv* in Iceland (though written *hv* still), e.g., O. N., O. Ic. *hvelva*, Norse *kvelva*. O. N. *ø* became *æ* in Iceland, *døma > dæma*. O. N. *æi* became *ei* in Iceland, e.g., O. N. *stæin >* O. Ic. *stein*, O. N. *bæin >* O. Ic. *bein* (*stin* and *bin* in O. Dan.).

9. Characteristics of Old Northumbrian.

The following are some of the chief differences between O. Nhb. and W. S:

1. Preference in O. Nhb. for *a* in many cases where W. S. has *e*.
2. *A* sometimes appears in closed syllable where W. S. has *æ*.

3. *A* before *l* + consonant is not broken to *ea* (Sievers § 121.3, and Lindelöf: Die Sprache des Durham Rituals).

4. *A* before *r* + consonant very frequently not broken, cp. *arm, farra*. Breaking occurs more often, however.

5. *E* before *l* + consonant not broken in the Ritual (see Lindelöf).

6. *E* before *r* + consonant is broken and appears as either *ea* or *eo*, cp. *eorthe, earthe*.

7. *A* before *h, ht, x (hs)* becomes *æ*. Sievers § 162.1. In W. S. *a* was broken to *ea*, cp. O. Nhb. *sax*, W. S. *seax*. This Lindelöf explains as due to the different quality of the *h*—in W. S. it was guttural, hence caused breaking; in Nhb. it was palatal and hence the preceding *a* was palatalized to *æ*.

8. Nhb. umlaut of *o* is *æ*. In W. S. it was *e*, cp. *dœma, sœca*, W. S. *dẹman, sẹcan*. See Sievers §§ 27 and 150.4. Bouterwek CXXVII, and Lindelöf. This difference was, however, levelled out, Nhb. *æ* becoming also *e*, according to Sievers.

9. Special Nhb. diphthongs *ei, ai*, cp. *heista, seista*, W. S. *hiehsta, siexta*.

10. Influence of preceding *w* was greater than in the South. A diphthong whose second element was a dark vowel was simplified generally to a dark vowel (Lindelöf), e.g., *weo > wo, wio > wu*, cp. *weorld > world, weord > word*, etc.

11. W. S. *t* is represented quite frequently by *ð* or *d*, regularly so when combined with *l*, often so when combined with *s*. See Lindelöf above.

12. W. S. *ð* frequently appears as *d* in the North; the reverse also occurs. See Bouterwek CXLII-CXLV. In a few cases *ð > t*.

13. *C* before *t* where W. S. regularly has *h*. See Bouterwek.

14. Metathesis of *r* less extensive than in W. S.

15. Preceding *g, c, sc* did not cause diphthongation in Nhb. as often as in W. S.

16. Generally speaking, less extensive palatalization in Nhb. than in W. S.

17. Dropping of final *n* in infinitives in Northumbrian.

10. Remarks. Metathesis of *r*.

The above characteristics of O. Nhb. will not only explain a great many later Scotch forms, but also show that a number of words which have been considered loanwords are genuine English. Sco. *daw*, "day," need not necessarily be traced to O. N. *dagr*. The W. S. *dæg* gave Eng. *day*. *Dæg* is also the Northern form. *Daw* may of course be due to *a* in the oblique cases, but according to 2 *dag* may have appeared in the nominative case early in the North. This would develop to *daw*. Sco. *daw*, verb, "to dawn," is easily explained. W. S. *dagian* > *dawn* regularly, Nhb. *dagia* (see 17 above) > *daw*. The O. N. *daga*, "to dawn," is then out of the question. Sco. *mauch*, "a kinsman"; the O. E. form was *mæg*, which would have given *may*. In the North the *g* was probably not palatal. Furthermore a Northern form *mag* would regularly develop to *maw*, might also be *mauch* (cp. *law* and *lawch*, adj., "low," O. N. *lagr*). O. N. *magr*, "kinsman," may, however, be the source of *mauch*. Sco. *hals* is not from O. N. *hals*, but from O. Nhb. *hals* which corresponded to W. S. *heals*; Sco. *hawse*, "to clasp," (Ramsay, II, 257); comes from O. Nhb. *halsiga*, W. S. *healsian*. (Sco. *hailse*, "to greet," is a different word, see loanword list, part II.). Forms that appear later in standard English frequently are found earliest in the North (cp. § 10). No. 13 explains some differences in the later pronunciation of Sco. and Eng. No. 12 is a characteristic that is much more common in Middle and Early New Scotch. Many words in this way became identical in form with their Norse cognates, cp. *broder, fad(d)er*, etc. This will be discussed later. No. 14, Metathesis of *r*, was carried out extensively in W. S. (see Sievers, 179), e.g., *beornan* "burn"; *iernan*, "run"; *burn*, "a stream"; *hors*, "horse"; *forsk*, "frog"; *þerscan*, "to thrash"; *berstan*, "to burst"; *fierst*, "a space of time," (cp. Norse *frist*, Germ. *Frist*). This progressive metathesis of *r* is very common in the South. In the North, on the contrary, metathesis of *r* has taken place before *ht* in *frohtian, fryhtu*, etc. (Sievers, 179, 2). In addition to these a large number of words appear in Old and Middle Sco. differing from literary English with regard to metathesis, sometimes showing metathesis where Eng. does not. A list of words will illustrate this difference: *thyrldom*, "thraldom"; *thirl*, "to enthrall"; *fryst*, "first"; *brest*, "to burst"; *thretty*, "thirty"; *thrid*, "third"; *thirl*, "to pierce thirl"; *gyrs*, "grass"; *krul*, "curl"; *drit*, "dirt"; *warsill*, "to wrestle"; *scart*, "to scratch"; *cruddled*, "curdled"; *birde*, O. E. *brid*, "offspring." The result is that many of these words are more like the corresponding O. N. words than the Anglo-Saxon (cp. O. N. *fristr*, *brenna*, Norse *tretti*, *tredie*, etc.), hence they have in many cases been considered loanwords. Sco. *braist* and *landbrest*, "breakers," (cp. O. N. *bresta*, *landbrest*), are not from the Norse but from the corresponding O. Nhb. words. *Cors* which occurs in Gau may be a similar case and like Eng. *cross* derived from O. Fr. *crois*, but Gau otherwise shows considerable Danish influence and Gau's form may be due to that. Eng. *curl* and *dirt* (from O. Du. *krul* and O. N. *drit*) have undergone metathesis. The Sco. words have not.

11. The Question of Palatalization in O. Nhb.

Just to what extent *g*, *c*, *sc* were palatalized in O. Nhb. is not definitely known. Until this has been ascertained the origin of a number of dialect words in the North will remain uncertain. The palatal character of *g*, *c*, *sc* in O. E. was frequently represented by inserting a palatal vowel, generally *e*, before the following guttural vowel. Kluge shows (in Litteraturblatt für germ, und rom. Philologie, 1887, 113-114) that the Middle English pronunciation of *crinჳen*, *sinჳen*, proves early palatalization, which was, however, not indicated in the writing of the O. E. words *cringan*, *singan*. And in the same way palatalization existed in a great many words where it was not graphically represented. Initial *sc* was always palatalized (Kluge, 114 above). In the MSS. *k* seems to represent a guttural, *c* a palatal sound of older *c* (Sievers, 207, 2). Palatalization of *c* is quite general. *K* became palatalized to *c* in primitive Eng. initially before front vowels, also before Gmc. *e* and *eu* (Kluge, P. G.[2] I, 991). Kluge accepts gutturalizing of a palatal *c* before a consonant where this position is the result of syncopation of a palatal vowel. In the South palatal *c* became a fricative *ch*. According to Kluge it never developed to *ch* in Northern England and Scotland, but either remained *c* or recurred to a guttural *k*. The same is true with regard to *g*. The exact extent of such palatalization is very difficult to determine. It is possible that the sound always remained a guttural in the North. We have seen that *c* or *g* did not cause diphthongation of the following vowel in the North as often as in the South. In view of the fact that palatalization was not always indicated, this may not prove anything, but may, however, indicate less palatalization than in the South. The fact that *e* or *i* was sometimes inserted before a following dark vowel, cp. *ahefgia*, "gravare," *gefragia*, "interrogare," proves that palatalization in these words, at least, existed.

12. *Sk* as a Scandinavian Sign.
Certain Words in *sk*. Palatalization in Norse.

Wall argues that non-palatalization cannot be regarded as a sign of Scand. influence and cites a number of words in support of this conclusion (see Wall, § 30). With regard to *dick*, "ditch," and *sag*, "sedge," Wall is probably right. Those in *sk* are, however, not so easily disposed of. The presence of certain words with *sk* in the South or those cited in *sh* in the North does not prove the case. While the presence of a word in South Eng. diall. is in favor of its genuine Eng. origin, it does not prove it, for certain words, undoubtedly Scand., are found in the Southern dialects. *Shag*, "rough hair," Skeat regards as Norse rather than Eng. *Scaggy*, "shaggy," with initial *sk*, I would regard as Norse from O. N. *skegg*, not from O. E. *sceagga*. *Shriek* Skeat regards as Scand. Bradley derives it from O. L. G. *scricon* which is found once in the Heliand. Eng. dial. *skrike*. Wall on the other hand derives it from O. E. *scricon*, since *scric* is found. *Scric* occurs in O. E. as the name of the shriekbird. The vb. is not found. Whether we regard "shriek" native or not, *scrike* is to be derived from O. N. *skrika*. *Skeer* is from O. N. *skera*; *sheer* from O. E.

sceran. In form if not in meaning, we have an exact parallel in the M. E. *skir*, "bright," from O. N. *skir*, and *schir* from O. E. *scir*. In a few cases words that seem Scand. appear with *sh*, not *sk*. The etymology of such words, however, becomes rather doubtful. This is especially the case where in the Norse word a guttural vowel followed the *sk*. Where, however, the Norse or Dan. word had a palatal vowel after the *sk* the change to *sh* is not at all impossible, and here arises the question of palatalization in O. N. O. N. *skiól*, pron. *sk-ióI*, with *sk*, = Norse *skjũl* (pron. *shũl*). *Ski* thus becomes *sh* in O. N. *skilinn*, Norse *shil*, O. N. *skilja*, Norse *shilja* (or *skille*), O. N. *skipta*, Norse *shifta*. West Norse also shows change of *k* to *ch* before *i* where the *k* has been kept in East Scand., e.g., O. Ic. *ekki* = W. Norse (dial.) *ikkje* or *intje*, pron. *ittje*, *intje*, Dan. *ikke* (*igge*). *I* between *sk* and a dark vowel early became *j* in Norse, which then gave the preceding *sk* something of a palatal nature. The development of O. N. *skiól* into *shiel* in Scotland and England may be explained in this way, as *skiól* > *shul* in Norway. This is, however, to be understood in this way, that if an *i* or *e* followed the *sk*, this was in condition to become palatalized, not that it was at all palatal at the time of borrowing. The sound was then distinctly guttural, and the guttural character of *sk* has in nearly every case been kept in Scand. loanwords in English, for palatalization of O. E. *sc* was completed before the period of borrowing. This palatalization of *sk* was general in Scotland as well as in England, and such words in *sk* must be regarded as Scand. loanwords.

13. Conclusion as to the Test of Non-palatalization.

As initial *sk*, corresponding to O. N. *sk*, O. E. *sc*, is due to Scand. influence, so, in general, medial and final *sk* may be also so regarded: cp. here Sco. *harsk*, "harsh," *bask* (adj.), *mensk*, *forjeskit*, etc. The guttural character of *g* and *k* in Sco. is not to be regarded as due to Scand. influence. Thus *mirk*, *reek*, *steek*, *streek*, *breek*, *dik*, *rike*, *sark*, *kirn*, *lig*, *brig*, *rig*, etc., are to be derived from the corresponding O. Nhb. words, not from O. N. There is something of uncertainty in these words, however, as they all could come from the O. N. O. N. *hryggr*, for instance, would become *rig* in Sco., just as would O. Nhb. *rycg* (*rygg*). O. N. *bryggia* would become *brig*, just as well as O. Nhb. *brycg* (*brygg*). The *i* after *g* in *bryggia* does not hinder this, since, as we know, the O. N. word was pronounced *brygg-ia*, not *bryddja*, as a later form would be.

14. Old and Middle Scotch.

After Chaucer, Northumbrian English became a mere popular dialect no longer represented in literature. But the form of Northumbrian spoken north of the Tweed, Lowland Scotch, has during the next three hundred years quite a different history. From the Scottish war of Independence to the Union of the Crowns, Scotland had its own literary language. It is customary to speak of three periods of Scottish language and literature as Old, Middle and New: Old Scotch extending down to about 1450; Middle Scotch to the Union of the Crowns; and New Scotch covering the period after the Union. This is, of course, simply a Northern and later form of the Northumbrian we have discussed above.

15. Some Characteristics of Scotch. O. E. ă, â.

There are no monuments in O. Sco. dating back to the 13th or first half of the 14th Century. The first of any importance that we have is "The Bruce" of 1375. By this time the language of Scotland had already undergone many changes that made its general character quite different from literary or Midland English. None of these changes tended so much to differentiate the two as the very different development of O. E. long and short *a*. In the south O. E. *a* > *ę* (*name* > *nēm* > *nęm*); but O. E. *â* > *ǭ*, later *ô* (*stân* > *stǭn* > *stône*, *hâm* > *hǭm* > *hôme*). The change of *â* to *ǭ* (probably about 1200) took place before that of *ă* to *â*, else they would have coincided and both developed to *ô* or *ç*. The last is precisely what took place in Scotland. O. Nhb. *ă* > *â* and early coincided with original *â*, and along with it developed to later *ç*, as only short *a* did in the south. The two appear together in rhyme in Barbour. Their graphic representation is *a*, *ai*, *ay*. The sound in Barbour is probably *æ* or *ę̄*. In "Wallace" Fr. *entré* is also written *entray*, *entra*. Fr. *a* and *ei* and Eng. diphthong *ai* (< *æg*) rhyme regularly with Sco. *a*, *ay*, *ai*, from O. E. *â*. On O. E. and O. N. *â*-and M. Sco. *ç*-sounds in general see Curtis, §§ 1-165.

16. Curtis's Table.

The following (see Curtis §§ 144-145) illustrates the development of O. E. *ă*, and *â*, in England and Scotland:

1. Central Scotland.	{ O. E. *ă* } { O. E. *â* }	> an *ç*-vowel.
2. S. Scotland and Ellis's D. 31² in England.	{ O. E. *ă* } { O. E. *â* }	> *ç* > an *i*-fracture in the mdn. diall.
3. The rest of Northern England and Midland.	O. E. *ă*	> an *ç*-vowel > *ç*, later *î*-fracture in D 25, 26, 28, 29.
4. Southern England	O. E. *â* > *ô* or *ŭ*, with fracture. O. E. *ă* > an *e*-fracture or *i*-fracture. O. E. *â* > *â* > *ŭ* or *ô*.	

In 1. O. E. *hâm* > *hçm*, *năme* > *nçm*.

In 2. *hâm* > *hçm* > *hiǝm*, *năme* > *nçm* > *niǝm*.

In 3. *hâm* > *hôm*, *hoǝm*, *hoŭm* or *hŭm* with fracture.

    năme > *nçm*.

    năme > *nçm* > *niǝm* in certain dialects.

In 4. *hâm* > *hŭm*, or *hom*.

    năme > *neǝm*, *niǝm*.

The intermediate stage of this development, however, is explained in two ways. According to Curtis it was (in 2) $\hat{a} > \bar{e} > ę > \hat{\imath} > i\partial$. Luik (§ 244) shows that

> das Vorrücken zum Vocalextrem ist an die Abstumpfung gebunden; wir finden es nur dort, wo auch Abstumpfung zu constatieren ist, wäbrend diese selbst ein weiteres Gebiet hat. Schon daraus folgt, dass die Abstumpfung das Primäre ist, dass also ihre Basis *e* war, nicht *i*. Dies wird bestätigt durch eine einfache Erwägung. Hätte die Abstumpfung die Lautstufe *i* ergriffen, so hätte sie auch das *e* treffen müssen, das ja schon seit Beginn der neuenglischen Zeit in allen Dialekten durch *i* vertreten ist. Endlich bieten die frühesten Zeugnisse nur *e*, nicht *i*, auch für solche Striche, die heute *i* haben.

According to this, then, the development is more probably $\tilde{a} > \bar{e} > ę\partial > i\partial$, or, as Luik thinks, $\tilde{a} > æ > æ\partial$, or $\bar{e}\partial > ę\partial > i\partial$

17. O. E. *ô.*—A List of Illustrative Words from the Aberdeen Dialect.

Another Northern peculiarity relates to O. E. *ô*. While in the south O. E. *ô* developed to an *ŭ*-vowel or an *ŭ*-fracture, in Scotland it became *ee* (*ui, ee, i*). The process involved here does not yet seem to be fully understood. The modern dialect of Aberdeen is most pronounced in this respect, older *i* also frequently becoming *u, o*. The following examples taken from "Johnnie Gibb" (Aberdeen. 1871) will illustrate:

1. Words with an *u* (o)-vowel in English that have *i* in Aberdeen dialect: *ither,* "other"; *mither,* "mother"; *tribble* (O. Fr. *troble*), "trouble"; *kwintra* (O. Fr. *contree*), "country"; *dis,* "does" (3. s. of "do"); *hiz,* "us"; *dizzen* (O. Fr. *dozaine*), "dozen"; *sipper* (O. Fr. *soper*), "supper." Here we may also include, *pit,* "to put"; *fit,* "foot." *Buik,*

"book," seems to show the intermediate stage, cp. also *tyeuk*, "took." On the other hand O. E. *broðer > breeder*; (*ge*)-*don > deen*; *judge* (O. Fr. *juger*) > *jeedge*, all of which have a short vowel in English recent speech.

2. Words with *ĭ* in Eng. that have *ŭ* in Aberdeen dialect: *full*, "to fill"; *spull*, "to spill"; *buzness* (cp. O. E. *bȳsig*), "business"; *wutness*, "witness"; *wull*, "will" (vb.); *wunna*, "will not"; *wutty*, "witty"; *chucken*, "chicken"; *fusky* (Gael. *usquebah*), "whiskey"; *sun*, "sin."

3. Words with *ôô* (or *iu*) in Eng. have *ee* (*î*) in Aberdeen dialect: *seer* (O. Fr. *sur*), "sure"; *seen*, "soon"; *refeese* (O. Fr. *refuser*), "refuse"; *peer* (O. Fr. *poure*), "poor"; *yeel* (M. E. ʒ*ole*), "yule"; *reed* (O. E. *rôd*), "rood"; *eese* (O. Fr. *us*), "use"; *shee* (O. E. *scço*), "shoe"; *adee*, "ado"; *tee*, "too"; *aifterneen*, "afternoon"; *skweel*, "school"; *reet* (O. E. *rôt*), "root"; *constiteetion*, "constitution." Cp. also *gweed* (O. E. *gôd*), "good." The *w* in *gweed*, *skweel*, shows again the process of change from *o* to *ee*. U in *buik* and *w* in *kwintra* also seem to represent the *u*-element that is left in the sound. In words like *refeese*, *keerious*, etc., where *ee* is from Fr. *u*, the sound is quite easily explained. So *fusky* from *usquebah*. *Full*, from O. E. *fyllan*, and *buzness* are interesting.

18. Inorganic *y* in Scotch.

Many words have developed a *y* where originally there was none. This phenomenon is, however, closely connected with *e-i*-fracture from original *â*. Y we find appears often before *a* (from original *â*). It is, then, simply the development of the *e-i*-fracture into a consonant + *a*, and may be represented thus: O. E. *âc* ("oak") > *ęc* > *çc* > *çɔc* > *iɔc* > *yak*. (See also Murray D.S.C.S., 105). Cp. *yance* and *yence*, "once"; *yell*, "ale"; *yak*, "ache." This also appears in connection with fracture other than that from O. E. *â*: cp. *yirth*, *yird*, for "earth."

19. *D* for the Spirant *th*.

This appears in a number of words: e.g., *ledder*, "leather"; *fader* (in Gau),*fadder*, "father"; *moder, mudder*, "mother"; *broder, brudder*, "brother"; *lidder* (A.S. *liðre*); *de* (Gau), "the" (article); *widdie* (O. E. *wiðig*), "withy"; *dead*, "death"; *ferde*, "fourth"; etc. In some works this tendency is quite general. Norse loanwords as a rule keep the spirant, but in the following loanwords *ð* has become *d*: *cleed, cleeding*, "clothe, clothing," from O. N. *klæða*; *red*, "to clear up," O. N. *ryðja*; *bodin*, O. N. *boðinn* (? See E.D.D.); *bud*, "bribe," O. N. *boð*; *heid*, "brightness," O. N. *hæið*; *eident*, "busy," O. N. *iðinn* (*ythand* is, however, the more common Sco. form); *bledder*, "to prate," O. N. *blaðra* (more commonly *blether* in Sco.); *byrd*, "ought," O. N. *burði*; *stiddy*, O. N. *steði*. I do not think *ryde*, "severe," can be derived from O. N. *reiðr*; and *frody*, "wise," is rather O. E. *frod* than O. N. *fróðr*. *Waith*, O. N. *væiðr*, has kept the spirant, but *faid*, a "company of hunters," has changed it to *d*. *Faid* probably comes in from Gaelic. I have called attention to this change of *ð* to *d* in Sco., since many words affected by it have become almost identical in form with their Scand. cognates and have consequently been considered loan-words. See § 23.

20. O. E. *â* and O. N. *æi*. How far we can Determine such Words to be of Native or of Norse Origin.

Certain Eng. dialect words in *ç* corresponding to O. E. *â* have been considered Scand. loanwords. We have, however, seen that in the north O. E. *â* > *ç* just as did O. N. *æi* (*ei*). How many of these words are genuine English and how many are loanwords becomes, then, rather uncertain. Wall argues that the Norse words were always in M. E. spelled with a diphthong, while the genuine English words were spelled with an *a*—thus *bain, baisk* from O. N. *bæinn, bæiskr*, but *hame, stane, hale* from O. E. *hâm, stân, hâl*. If this were always the case we should have here a safe test. It is, however, a fact that in Scottish texts at least, no such consistency exists with regards to these words. The following variant spellings will show this: *hame, haim, haym; stain, stane, stayne; hal, hale, hail, hayle; lak, lake, laik, layk; blake, blaik, blayk*, etc., etc. There is, however, another way in which to determine which of such words are loanwords and which are not. In Southern Scotland in D. 33, and in Northwestern England (D. 31), O. N. *æi* and O. E. *â* did not coincide, but have been kept distinct down to the present time (see Ellis's word-lists and Luik, 220, 221). In these two dialects O. E. *â* developed to an *i*-fracture (see § 16.2), while O. N. *æi* never went beyond the *e*-stage, and remains an *e*-vowel in the modern dialects. Here, then, we have a perfectly safe test for a large number of words. Those that have in D. 31 and D. 33 an *i*-vowel or an *i*-fracture are genuine English, those that have an *e*-vowel are Scandinavian loanwords. Ellis's list offers too few examples of words of this class. We find *hi'm, bi'n, hi'l, sti'n*, and in Murray's D.S.C.S. *heame*, and *heale* (beside *geate* (O. N. *gata*), *beath, meake, tweae, neame*, etc.). This then proves that Sco. *haim, bain, hail*, and *stain* are from O. E. *hâm, bân, hâl, stân* and not from O. N. *hæim, bæinn, hæil, stæinn. Mair*, in spite of its *e*-vowel, is not from O. N. *mæir*, for a following *r* prevented the development to *i*, as a rule, although in Cumberland *meear* is found beside *mair*. The word "steak" (O. N. *stæik*), which occurs in Ellis's list, has had an irregular development and cannot be considered here (see further Luik, 323). In the following works are found a number of words of this class:

Westmoreland and Cumberland Dialects, by J.R. Smith. London. 1839.

A Glossary of Words and Phrases of Cumberland, by William Dickinson. London. 1859.

Folk Speech of Cumberland, by Alexander Craig Gibson. London. 1873.

A Glossary of Words used in Swaledale, Yorkshire, by John Harand. E.D.S. 1873.

Whitby Glossary, by F.K. Robinson. E.D.S. 1876.

21. A List of Some Words that are Norse. Further Remarks.

These all aim at giving the phonetic value of the sounds. O. E., O. N. *â* is represented by *ea* or *eea*, indicating *i*-fracture. For instance: *heam, steean, neam, geat, beeath, leath* (O. N. *laði*), *heeal, brea* (O. N. *brâ*), *breead* (O. E. *brâd*, not O. N. *bræi*), *greeay, blea*, etc. Those that have *a, ai,* or *ay*, that is an *e*-vowel, and must consequently be derived from the corresponding O. N. words, are the following:

blake, *adj.* yellow, pale, O. N. *blæikr*.

blaken, *vb.* to turn yellow, N.N. *blæikna*.

clame, *vb.* to adhere, O. N. *klæima*.

clam, *adj.* slimy, deriv.

claming, *sb.* adhesive material, deriv.

flay, *vb.* to frighten, O. N. *fleya*.

flaytly, *adv.* timidly, deriv.

hain, *vb.* to save, protect, O. N. *hegna*.

lake, laike, *vb.* to play, O. N. *læika*, cp. O. E. *lâcan*.

lakeing, *sb.* a toy, deriv.

lave, *sb.* the remainder, O. N. *læifr*, cp. O. E. *lâf*.

rate, *vb.* to bleach, whiten, O. N. *rôyta*. M. L. G. *roten*, is out of the question, and *reeat would be the form corresponding to M. L. G. *raten*.

slake, *vb.* to smear, daub, O. N. *slæikja*. O. L. G. *slikken* does not correspond.

slake, *sb.* a kiss, deriv., cp. O. N. *slæikr*.

slape, *adj.* slippery, O. N. *slæipr*, cp. O. E. *slape*.

slapen, *vb.* to make smooth, O. N. *slæipna*, but possibly deriv. from *slape*.

snape, *vb.* to restrain, O. N. *snöypa*.

In addition to these, *blain*, "to become white," is a Scand. loan-word, but rather from Dan. *blegne* than Norse *blœikna*, cp. *blake* above. *Blained*, adj. "half dry," said of linen hung out to dry, is, of course, simply the pp. of *blain*, cp. Dan. *blegned*. *Skaif*, "distant, wild, scattered abroad, or apt to be dispersed" (is the definition given), corresponds exactly to O. N. *skœif* in form, but not in meaning. *Skœif* meant "crooked." Sco. *daive*, "to stun, stupefy," is here regularly spelled *deeave* (*deave* in Swaledale). It must, then, be derived from O. E. *deafian*, not O. N. *döyfa*, O. Ic. *deyfa*. Swaledale *slaiching*, "sneaking," is the same as O. N. *slœikja*, "to lick"; a secondary meaning of O. N. *slœikja* is "to sneak"; *keeal*, "kail," could come from O. N. *kál* or Gael. *cál*. It is probably from the latter. The word *slaister*, "to dawdle, to waste one's time," is not clear. The sb. *slaisterer*, "a slink, an untidy person," is also found. The *ai* indicates an original diphthong. It is probably the same as Norse *slöysa*, sb. "an untidy person," as vb. "to be untidy, to be careless." *Ster* (*slais* + *ster*) would, then, be an Eng. suffix, or it may be the same as that in Sco. *camstary*, cp. Germ. *halsstarrig*. The Norse word *slöysa* is probably not the direct source of the Eng. dialect word. *Slaister*, however, for *slöysa*, seems to be a recent word in Norse. *Skane*, "to cut the shell fish out of the shell" (Wall, list B), is to be derived from O. N. *skœina*, rather than from O. E. *scœnan*. *Slade*, "breadth of greensward in plowed land," cannot be from O. N. *slettr*, "plain," *sletta*, "a plain." Neither form nor meaning quite correspond. The Sw. *slägd* corresponds perfectly in form but not in meaning. It is, however, probably from O. E. *slæd*. This word is taken from Wall's list, not from the works named above.

22. Celtic, Lowland Scotch, and Norse.

In Gaelic and Irish, in the Western Isles and the Highlands, considerable Norse elements are found as the result of Norse occupancy that continued in the Isles, at least, for several hundred years. A number of words that have come into Gaelic and Irish from Norse are also found in Lowland Scotch. In some cases it seems that the word has not come into Lowland Scotch direct from Norse, but by way of Gaelic or Irish. Craigie has given a list of about 200 words in Gaelic that seem to come from Norse. Out of these I will take a few that have corresponding words in Scotch:

GAELIC OR IRISH.	LOWLAND SCOTCH.	OLD NORSE.
gardha	garth	garðr
lobht	loft	loft
prine	prin	prjónn
stop	stoup	staup
sgeap	skep	skeppa
sainseal	hansell	handsal
gaort	girt, girth	giörð
cnapp, cneap	knap	knappr
maol	mull	múli
sgeir	sker	sker
scarbh	scarth	scarfr
gead	ged, gedde	gedda
scát	scait	skata
brod	brod	broddr
masg	mask Dan.	maske
rannsaich	ransack, runsick	rannsaka

Garth and loft agree perfectly with the O. N. and are not doubtful. With the Gael. gardh cp. O. N. garðr and O. Sw. gardher. The Sco. garth has changed the original voiced spirant to a voiceless one. In Gael. lobht f has become v. Prin is rather doubtful. There is an O. E. prçon from which the Gael. word may have come. The Sco. word prin does not seem to come from either O. E. prçon or O. N. prjónn, but from the Gael. prine. There is a Northern dialectic prçon which may come from O. E. prçon. There is also a pren in Dan. dial. Stoup has the Norse diphthong which has been simplified in Gael. stop. Skep is a little doubtful because of meaning. The loanword sgeap in Gael. has the specialized meaning of "a beehive." This meaning the Sco. word has very frequently, the Norse to my knowledge never. It may be a case of borrowed meaning from Gael. *Girth* is from the Norse. *Girt* is probably simply change of *th* to *t*, which is also found elsewhere in Sco. *Knap* may be from either. *Mull* in Sco. may be native English. The word occurs in L. G. *Sker* is from O. N. *Skarth* is anomalous, showing change of *f* to *th*. In the Gael. *scarbh*, *f* is changed to *v* as in *lobht*. *Ged* is nearer the O. N. *Scait* could be from either, as also *brod*. Sco. *mask* is probably not at all a loanword, and may be from older *mex* by metathesis of *s*; cp. O. E. *mexfat* and Sco. *maskfat* cited by Skeat, Et. Dict. The Gael. *masg* is probably not a loanword from the Scand., but from O. E., or perhaps from O. Sco. An O. Nhb. *mesk* probably existed. *Ransack* agrees with the Norse word. The spelling *runsick* found once (Wallace VII, 120), probably does not represent the exact sound, and is, in any case, as *ransack* to be derived from the O. N. and not through the Gael. *Faid*, "a company of hunters," has already once been referred to. This cannot possibly come from the O. N. *væiðr*, for while the spirant *ð* sometimes becomes *d*, O. N. *v* regularly becomes *w* in Sco. (rarely *v*). We should expect the form *waith*, and this is the form we have in Wallace I, 326, in the sense "the spoil of the chase." There is a Gael. *fiadhoig*, meaning "a huntsman." The first element *fiad* seems to be the O. N. *veiðr* with regular change of *ð* to *d* (or *dh*, cp. *gardha*), and *v* or *w* to *f* which is considered a sign of Gael. influence in Aberdeen Sco., cp. *fat* for *what*, *fen* for *when*, etc., the development probably being *wh* > *w* > *v* > *f*. *Faid* in Sco. is then probably from the Gaelic.

23. Some Words that are not Scandinavian Loanwords.

We have spoken in §§ 10, 13, 20 and 22, of a number of words that are to be considered regular Sco. developments of O. E. words. The following words have also generally been derived from the Scand., but must be considered native, or from sources other than Norse:

Blait, *adj.* backward, must be traced to O. E. *blçat*, rather than to O. N. *blout*. O. N. *ou*, *au* is always *ou* or *oi* in Sco.

Breid, *sb.* breadth, not Norse *bræidde* nor Dan. *bredde*, but native Eng.

Cummer, *sb.* misery, wail, seems uncertain. It corresponds in form and usage exactly to Norse *kummer*, but *mb > mm* is natural and occurs elsewhere in Sco., cp. *slummer*, "slumber," which need not be derived from Norse *slummer* or any L. G. word. The usage of the word is peculiarly Scand.

Dead, *sb.* death. Not Dan.-Norse *död*, but English "death."

Fald, *vb.* to fall. Skeat says the *d* is due to Scand. influence, but cp. *boldin* from *bolna* (older *bolgna*). So *d* after *l* in *fald* may be genuine. Besides the O. N. word is *falla*, later Dan. *falde*.

Ferde, ordinal of four, not Norse *fjerde*. See § 19.

Flatlyngis, *adv.* flatly, headlong, looks very much like Norse *flatlengs* and corresponds perfectly in meaning. The Norse word is, however, a late formation, apparently, and *-lyngs* is a very common adverbial ending in Sco.

Hap, *vb.* to cover up, to wrap up, cannot come from O. Sw. *hypia*, as *y* could not become *a*.

Ledder, *sb.* leather. Not from Dan. *leder*, for cp. § 19; besides the vowel in the Dan. word is long.

Mister, *sb.* and *vb.* need, from O. Fr. *mestier*, not from O. N. *miste*, which always means "to lose," as it does in the modern diall. The O. Fr. *mestier* meant "office, trade," and sometimes "need." The last is the meaning of the modern *métier* in the dialects of Normandy. Both meanings exist in Northern English.

Ouke, *sb.* week. In all probability from O. E. *wucu* by loss of initial *w* before *u*. The Dan. *uge* does not quite correspond. The O. N. *vika* even less. The Danish *uge* simply shows similar dropping of *w* (*v*) as the Sco. word.

Rigbane, *sb.* backbone. Both elements are Eng. The compound finds a parallel in Norse *rygbæin*.

Soom, *vb.* to swim. Not Dan. *sömme*, but loss of *w* before *oo*, cp. the two Norse forms *svömma* and *symma*. Cp. *soote*, the last word in the first line of the Prologue to Chaucer's Canterbury Tales.

Teem, *vb.* to empty. It is not necessary to derive this from Norse *tömme*, "to empty." There is an O. E. *tôm* from which the Sco. adj. *toom* probably comes. *Toom* is also a verb in Sco. *Teem* is simply this same word by characteristic Sco. change of *o* to *e*. (See § 17.) This also explains the length of the vowel.

Trak, *vb.* to pull, not necessarily Norse *trekka*, cp. the L. G. *trekken*.

Wid, *sb.* wood. Not O. N. *viðr* nor Dan. *ved*. The vowel is against it in both cases. But just as above *toom* becomes *teem*, so *wood* > *wid*, cp. Sco. *guid*, "good," *pit*, "put," etc. (See § 17.) Hence also the shortness of the vowel in *wid*.

Were, *sb.* spring, cp. Latin *ver*. *Var, vaar* in Scand. does not account for the *e* in the Sco. word.

Yird, *sb.* earth. Not from Dan. *jord*. See next word.

Yirth, *sb.* earth, an inorganic *y* (see § 18). Not from O. N. *jörð*. For *d* in *yird* see § 19.

24. Loanword Tests.

I have adopted the following tests of form, meaning and distribution in determining the Scand. source of loanwords:

1. The diphthong *ou, ow* corresponding to O. N. *ou*, O. E. *ea*.
2. *Ai, ay* corresponding to O. N. *æi*, O. E. *â* as far as such words can be determined from modern dialects according to § 20.
3. The spirant *th* corresponding to O. N. *ð*, and O. E. *d*.
4. Consonantal assimilation of *nk* to *kk*, *mb* to *bb*, *mp* to *pp*, *ðl* to *ll*, *ʒd* and *rd* to *dd*, corresponding to similar assimilation in Scand.
5. Other consonantal and inflexional forms that are Scand., as opposed to O. Nhb. *d* for Scand. *d*, O. E. *ð* excluded, see §§ 19 and 23.

6. A word that is used in a sense distinctively Scand., as opposed to Eng. or L. G., is to be regarded as a loanword.
7. The distribution of a word in South England diall., or in O. F., O. S. or M. L. G., indicates that the word is not a Scand. loanword.
8. On the other hand, if a word occurs exclusively in Scand. settlements in England and Scotland, it is to be regarded as due to Scand. influence in Scotch in spite of L. G. parallels.
9. The presence of a word in O. E. excludes Scand. influence, except in cases where the O. E. word has been shown to be a loanword. See Steenstrup and Kluge.

25. Remarks on the Texts.

The following dates it may be well to remember:

Barbour's "Bruce" finished about 1375.
Wyntoun's Chronicle written about 1420.
Henry the Minstrel's "Wallace" written about 1450.
Dunbar lived from 1460 to 1520.
Douglas lived from 1475 to 1520.
Sir David Lyndsay lived from 1490 to 1555.
Alexander Scott lived from 1547 to 1584.
"The Complaynt of Scotland" was written about 1549.
Alexander Montgomery lived from 1540 to 1610.
Allan Ramsay lived from 1686 to 1758.
Robert Burns lived from 1759 to 1796.

"The Bruce," Wyntoun's "Cronykale" and the "Wallace" belong, then, to the early period of Scotch, which, for convenience, has been called Old Scotch. The last half of the 15th Century is a transition period. The language of Dunbar and Douglas is already Middle Scotch. Middle Scotch of the 16th Century is further represented by Lyndsay, Alexander Scott and Montgomery. "The Complaynt of Scotland" is Central Scotch of the middle of the 16th Century. Ramsay represents Early New Scotch. The language of Burns is in all essentials present Scotch. From the Scottish War of Independence down to the Union of the Crowns the literary standard of Scotland was Central Scotch. After the Union there was no longer a Scotch language of literature and Central Scotch became a mere spoken dialect like the other dialects of Scotland. The writings of Ramsay and Burns represent local dialects just as the large number of Scotch dialect writers of the last and this century have written in their own peculiar local vernacular. The great majority of loanwords are taken from "The Bruce," "The Wallace," Douglas, Dunbar, Scott and Montgomery. "The Bruce" has a large number of Scand. elements; it represents, however, literary Scotch and not Aberdeen Scotch of 1375. "Johnnie Gibb," written in modern Aberdeen dialect, has not a very large Scand. element, while "Mansie Wauch" (modern Edinburgh dialect) has a far larger number. In "The Wallace" Scand. elements are quite prominent. So in the writings of Douglas, Scott and Montgomery. "The Complaynt of Scotland" has comparatively very few loanwords from Scand., while on the other hand the French element is more prominent than in the other works. Norse elements are not prominent in Lyndsay. None of the Scotch writers has as many Scand. words as Dunbar. We may say that they are nearly as prominent in Dunbar's works as in the Ormulum, Midland English of about 300 years before Dunbar's works were written.

The numbers given in the references are self-explanatory. They are generally to page and line, in some cases to book and verse, as in Bruce and Wyntoun. T.W.M. refers to Dunbar's "Twa Mariit Wemen." F. to "The Flyting with Kennedy." F. after Montgomery's name refers to "The Flyting." G.T. refers to Dunbar's "Golden Targe," and C. and S. to Montgomery's "Cherrie and the Slae." M.P. to the "Miscellaneous Poems" and S. to the "Sonnets."

Only words that are specifically Scotch in form or usage have been included. Very well known Scotch words, that occur in older Scotch as well as the modern dialects, such as *blether*, *busk*, *ettle*, *kilt*, etc., are given without references to texts where they have been found, otherwise one or more references are given in each case. For the sake of comparison and illustration Shetland and Cumberland forms are frequently given. Wherever a W. Scand. source is accepted fora loanword the O. N. form is given if it be different from O. Ic. Examples from Danish dialects or Swedish dialects are given as Dan. dial. or Sw. dial. Those from Norse dialects are cited as Norse simply. Those that are specifically literary Norse are cited as Dano-Norse.

PART II.

LOANWORDS.

Agait, *adv.* uniformly. R.R. 622. Sco. *ae*, one, + O. N. *gata* literally "ae way," one way.

Agait, *adv.* astir, on the way. See Wall.

Agrouf, *adv.* on the stomach, grovelling. Ramsay, II, 339. O. N. *á grúfu*, id. See *grouf.*

Airt (ĕrt), *vb.* urge, incite, force, guide, show. O. N. *erta*, to taunt, to tease, *erting*, teasing. Norse *erta, örta*, id. Sw. dial. *erta*, to incite some one to do a thing. Sw. *reta* shows metathesis. M. E. *ertin*, to provoke.

Allgat, *adv.* always, by all means. Bruce, XII, 36; L.L. 1996. O. N. *allu gatu.* O. Ic. *öllu gǫtu*. See Kluge, P. G.² I., 938.

Algait, algatis, *adv.* wholly. Douglas, II, 15, 32; II, 129, 31. See Kluge, P. G.² I., 938.

Althing, as a *sb.* everything. Gau, 8, 30, corresponding to Dan. *alting.* "Over al thing," Dan. *over alting.* Not to be taken as a regular Sco. word, however. Gau has a number of other expressions which correspond closely to those of the Dan. original of Kristjern Pedersen, of which Gau's work is a translation.

Anger, *sb.* grief, misery. Bruce, I, 235. Sco. Pro. 29. O. N. *angr*, grief, sorrow. See Bradley's Stratmann, and Kluge and Lutz. The root *ang* is general Gmc., cp. O. E. *angmod*, "vexed in mind." M. L. G. *anxt*, Germ. *angst*, Dan. *anger.* The form of the word in Eng., however, is Scand.

Angryly, *adv.* painfully. Wyntoun, VI, 7, 30. Deriv., cp. Cu. *angry*, painful, O. N. *angrligr*, M. E. *angerliche*. The O. Dan. vb. *angre*, meant "to pain," e.g., *thet angar mek, at thu skal omod thorn stride* (Kalkar).

Apert, *adj.* bold. Bruce, XX, 14. *apertly*, boldly, XIV, 77. Evidently from O. N. *apr*, sharp, cp. *en aprasta hrið*, "sharp fighting," cited in Cl. and V. Cl. and V. compares N. Ic. *napr*, "snappish," cp. furthermore *apirsmert*, adj. (Douglas, II, 37, 18), meaning "crabbed," the second element of which is probably Eng. *Apr* in O. N. as applied to persons means "harsh, severe" (Haldorson).

Assil-tooth, *sb.* molar tooth. Douglas, I, 2, 12. See Wall.

At, *conj.* that. O. N. *at*, Norse, Dan. *at*, to be regarded as a Scand. word. Might in some places be due to Celtic influence, but its early presence, and general distribution in Scand. settlements in England, Scotland, Shetland, etc., indicates that it is Scand.

Aweband, *sb.* "a band used for tying cattle to the stake." Jamieson, Lothian. O. N. *há-band*, "vinculum nervos poplitis adstringens" (Haldorson). Norse *habbenda*, "to tie cattle with a rope between the knees to keep them from running away." Cp. O. Sw. *haband*, Sw. dial. *haband*, "a rope that unites the oar with the oarlock."

Awkwart, *prep.* athwart, across. Wallace, III, 175; II, 109. Same as the Eng. adj. "awkward" which was originally an adv. Etymologically it is the O. N. *afugr* (O. Ic. *öfugr*) + Eng. *ward* (Skeat), cp. the Norse vb. *afvige*, to turn off. I have not found the prepositional use of the word in Eng. Cp. "toward."

Awsome, *adj.* terrible, deriv. from *awe* (O. N. *ági*). The ending *some* is Eng. O. N. *ágasamr*, Norse *aggsam*, means "turbulent, restless."

Aynd (çnd), *sb.* O. N. *andi*, breath, O. Sw. *ande*, Norse *ande*, Dan. *aande*.

Aynding, *sb.* breathing, deriv. See *aynd*.

Ayndless, *adj.* breathless. Bruce, X, 609. See *aynd*.

Bait, *vb.* to incite. Dunbar, 21127. O. N. *bæita*, O. Ic. *beita*. See B-S.

Baith, bath (bçth), *pron.* both. M. E. *bôþe*, *bâþe*, Cu. *beatth*, Eng. *both*, O. N. *bâðir*, O. Dan. *bâðe*. Skeat.

Baittenin, *pr. p.* thriving. Jamieson. O. N. *batna*, Eng. *batten*. See Skeat, and Kluge and Lutz.

Baittle (bçtl), *sb.* a pasture, a lea which has thick sward of grass. Jamieson, Dumfries. O. N. *bæita*, "to feed," *bæiti*, pasturage. Cp. Norse *fjellbæite*, a mountain pasture.

Ban, *vb.* to swear, curse. Dunbar, 13, 47; Rolland, II, 680. O. N. *banna*, to swear, to curse, *banna*, a curse, Norse *banna*, to swear, *banning*, swearing, W. Sw. dial. *bænn* id., Dan. *bande*, to swear, to wish one bad luck, O. S. *banna* id. M. Du. *bannen* means to excommunicate. This is the L. G. meaning. The Sco. usage is distinctly Scand. It is also a Northern word in Eng. diall. Cp. Shetland *to ban*, to swear.

Bang, *vb.* to beat. Sat. P. 39, 150. O. N. *banga*, O. Sw. *banka*, Norse, *banke*, to beat, to strike. Cp. Shetland *bonga*, in "open de door dat's a bonga," somebody is knocking, literally "it knocks" Norse *det banka*. *Bang* is very frequently used in the sense of rushing off, cp. Dalrymple's translation of Leslie, I, 324, 7.

Bangster, *sb.* a wrangler. Sat. P. 44, 257. Evidently Norse *bang* + Eng. suffix *ster*. See *bang* vb. Cp. *camstarrie*, where the second syllable corresponds to that in Germ. *halsstarrig*.

Bark, *vb.* to tan, to harden. Dunbar F. 202 and 239. Ramsay, I, 164, "barkit lether," tanned leather. O. N. *barka*, to tan, Norse *barka*, to tan, to harden, M. E. *barkin*. General Scand. both sb. and vb. In the sense "to tan" especially W. Scand., cp. Sw. *barka*, to take the bark off. O. Sw. *barka*, however, has the meaning "to tan."

Barknit, *adj.* clotted, hardened. Douglas, II, 84, 15. pp. of vb. *barken*, to tan. See above.

Bask, *adj.* dry, withering (of wind). Jamieson, Dumfries. Dan. *barsk*, hard, cold, *en barsk Vinter*, a cold winter. Cp. Sco. "a bask daw," a windy day. M. L. G. *barsch* and *basch* do not agree in meaning with the Sco.

word; besides the *sk* is Scand. For loss of *r* before *sk* cp. *hask* from *harsk.*

Bauch, bawch, baugh, *adj.* awkward, stiff, jaded, disconsolate, timid. Sat. P. 12, 58; Dunbar Twa. M.W. 143; Rolland, IV, 355; Johnnie Gibb, 127, 2. O. N. *bagr,* awkward, clownish, inexperienced, unskilful. *Bauchly,* poorly, in Ramsay, II, 397.

Bayt, *vb.* to feed, graze. Bruce, XIII, 589, 591; Lyndsay, 451, 1984. O. N. *bæit,* to feed, to graze, causative from *bita,* literally means to make to bitE. Norse *bita,* to graze, Sw. *beta,* M. E. *beyten.* In many diall. in Norway the word means "to urge, to force." Cp. *bait.*

Beck, *sb.* a rivulet, a brook. Jamieson. O. N. *bekkr,* O. Sw. *bäkker,* Norse *bekk,* O. Dan. *bæk.* Sw. *bäck,* a rivulet. In place-names a test of Scand. settlements.

Beet, *vb.* to incite, inflame. Burns, 4, 8. Same as *bait,* incite, q.v. Cp. Cu. "to beet t'yubm, to supply sticks, etc. to the oven while heating" (Dickinson).

Big, begg, *sb.* barley. Fergusson, II, 102; Jamieson, Dumfries. O. N. *bygg,* Dan. *byg.* See Wall. Cp. Shetland *big.*

Begrave, *vb.* to bury. Douglas, II, 41, 25; IV, 25, 22; IV, 17, 8. Dan. *begrave,* Norse *begrava,* O. Sw. *begrava, begrafwa,* to bury. Possibly not a loanword.

Bein, bene, bein, *adj.* liberal, open-handed, also comfortable, pleasant. Douglas, III, 260, 23; Fergusson, 108; Sat. P. 12, 43. *Beine,* hearty, in Philotus, II, is probably the same word. O. N. *bæinn.*

Beir, *vb.* to roar. Douglas, II, 187, 1. See *bir,* sb.

Big, *vb.* to build, dwell, inhabit. Dunbar T.M.W. 338; Dalr., I, 26, 19; Sco. pro. 5. O. N. *byggia.* See Wall. Sco. "to big wi' us," to live with us, cp. Norse *ny-byddja,* to colonize.

Bigging, bygine, *sb.* a building. O. N. *bygging,* a building, habitation. Scand. diall. all have the form *bygning,* so O. Sw. *bygning.* The word may be an independent Sco. formation just as *erding,* "burial," from *erde,* "to bury"; *layking,* "a tournament," from *layke,* "to sport"; *casting,* "a cast-off garment," from *cast*; *flytting*, "movable goods," from *flyt*, "to move"; *hailsing*, "a salute," from *hailse*; and Eng. *dwelling*, "a house," from vb. *dwell*. Cp. however Shetland *bogin*.

Bing, *sb.* a heap, a pile. Douglass, II, 216, 8. O. N. *bingr*, a heap, O. Sw. *binge*. Norse *bing* more frequently a heap or quantity of grain in an enclosed space. O. Dan. *byng, bing*.

Bir, birr, beir, *sb.* clamor, noise, also rush. S. S. 38; Lyndsay, 538, 4280. O. N. *byrr*, a fair wind. O. Sw. *byr*. Cp. Cu. *bur* and Shetland "a pirr o' wind," a gust. Also pronounced *bur, bor*.

Birring, *pr. p.* flapping (of wings). Mansie Wauch, 159, 33. See *bir*.

Bla, blae (blç), *adj.* blue, livid. Douglas, III, 130, 30; Irving, 468. O. N. *blá*, blue, Norse *blaa, blau*, Sw. *blå*, Dan. *blaa*. Not from O. E. *blço*.

Blabber, *vb.* to chatter, speak nonsense. Dunbar F., 112. O. N. *blabbra*, lisp, speak indistinctly, Dan. *blabbre* id., Dan. dial. *blabre*, to talk of others more than is proper. M. E. *blaber*, cp. Cu. *blab*, to tell a secret. American dial. *blab*, to inform on one, to tattle. There is a Gael. *blabaran*, sb. a stutterer, which is undoubtedly borrowed from the O. N. The meaning indicates that.

Blaik, *vb.* to cleanse, to polish. Johnnie Gibb, 9, 6. O. N. *blæikja*, to bleach, O. Sw. *blekia*, Sw. dial. *bleika*. All these are causative verbs like the Sco. The inchoative corresponding to them is *blæikna* in O. N., N.N., *blekna* in O. Sw., *blegne* in Dan. See *blayknit*. Cp. Shetland *bleg*, sb. a white spot.

Blayknit, *pp.* bleached. Douglas, III, 78, 15. O. N. *blæikna*, to become pale, O. Sw. *blekna*, Norse *blæikna* id. O. N. *blæikr*, pale. Cp. Cu. *blake*, pale, and *bleakken* with *i*-fracture. O. E. *blâc, blæcan*.

Bleck, *vb.* put to shame. Johnnie Gibb, 59, 34, 256, 13. O. N. *blekkja*, to impose upon, *blekkiliga*, delusively, *blekking*, delusion, fraud; a little doubtful.

Blether, bledder, *vb.* to chatter, prate. O. N. *blaðra*, to talk indistinctly, *blaðr*, sb. nonsense. Norse *bladra*, to stammer, to prate, Sw. dial. *bladdra*, Dan. dial. *bladre*, to bleet. Cp. Norse *bladdra*, to act foolishly.

Blether, *sb.* nonsense. Burns 32, 2, 4 and 4, 2, 4. O. N. *blaðr*, nonsense. Probably the Sco. word used substantively.

Blome, *sb.* blossom. Bruce, V, 10; Dunbar, I, 12. Same as Eng. *bloom* from O. N. *blómi*.

Blome, *vb.* to flourish, successfully resist. Douglas, IV, 58, 25. "No wound nor wapyn mycht hym anis effeir, forgane the speris so butuus blomyt he." Small translates "show himself boastfully." The word *blómi* in O. N. used metaphorically means "prosperity, success."

Blout, blowt, *adj.* bare, naked, also forsaken. Douglas, III, 76, 11; IV, 76, 6. O. N. *blautr*, Norse *blaut*, see Cl. and V. The corresponding vowel in O. E. is *ea*: *blçat*. The O. N. as well as the N.N. word means "soft." The O. E. word means "wretched." In Sco. *blout* has coincided in meaning with *blait*. The Dan. word *blot* is, on account of its form, out of the question.

Bodin, *adj.* ready, provided. Douglas, III, 22, 24; Dunbar, 118, 36; Wyntoun, VII, 9, 213. From *boðinn*, *boðja* (E.D.D.).

Bolax, *sb.* hatchet. Jamieson. O. N. *bolöx*, a poleaxe, Norse *bolöks*, O. Sw. *bolöxe*, *bolyxe*, O. Dan. *bulöx*, Dano-Norse *bulaks*. Ormulum *bulaxe* (see further Brate).

Bole, *sb.* the trunk of a tree. Isaiah, 44, 19. O. N. *bolr*, the trunk of a tree, Norse *bol*, *bul*, O. Sw. *bol*, *bul*, Sw. dial. *bol* id.

Boldin, *vb.* to swell. Douglas, II, 52; I, II, 130, 25. Norse *bolna*, older *bolgna*, Dan. *bolne*, M. E. *bollen* (also *bolnin*). The Sco. word has developed an excrescent *d* after *l*. In Lindsay, 127, 3885, *boildin*, adj. pp. swollen.

Bolle, *sb.* a measure. Bruce, III, 221; Wyntoun, VII, 10, 519, 521, 523. O. N. *bolli*, a vessel, *blotbolli*, a measure, Sw. *bulle*. Rather than from O. E. *bolla* (Eng. *bowl*).

Boun, *adj.* bent upon, seems to have almost the idea of "compelled to." Gol. and Gaw. 813. O. N. *búinn*. See Wall under *bound*, and Cl. and V. under *bua* B. II.

Boune, *vb.* to prepare, to prepare to go, to go. Houlate, I, 23; Poet. R. 107, I; Gol. and Gaw. 59, 13, 40. See *bown*.

Bowdyn, *pp. adj.* swollen. Dunbar T.M.W. 41, 345; Montg. F. 529. See *boldin.*

Bowk, *sb.* trunk of the body, body. Dunbar, 248, 25; Rolland, II, 343. O. N. *búkr,* the trunk, the body, Norse *búk,* Dan. *bug,* O. Sw. *buker.* Specific Scand. usage. O. E. *búc,* like O. F. *buk* and Germ. *bauch,* meant "belly."

Bow, *sb.* a fold for cows. Douglas, III, 11, 4. O. N. *ból,* a place where cows are penned, also den, lair or lying-place of beasts. Norse *bol,* Shetland *bol, bøl,* a fold for cattle. In Psalms XVII, 12, *bole* occurs in the sense of "a lion's den."

Bown, *adj.* ready, prepared. L.L. 1036. O. N. *búinn.* Not Eng., but a loanword from O. N., and as Kluge P. G.² I, 939, has pointed out shows also Norse influence in the Midland dial.

Bowne, *vb.* to swell. Irving, 230. O. N. *bolgna* to swell, Norse *bolna,* Dan. *bolne.* Shows characteristic Sco. change of *l* to *w.* In *boudin,* Irving, 467, an excrescent *d* has developed before the *l* became *u* (*w*). Wallace, VI, 756, *bolnyt,* swelled. So in Wyntoun, IX, 17, 5. *Boldnit* with excrescent *d* occurs in Douglas, II, 84, 16.

Bra, brae, bray (brç), a slope, declivity. O. N. *brá,* see Bradley's Stratmann. Cp. *Jöstedalsbrä* in Western Norway.

Braid (brçd), *sb.* a sudden movement, an assault (Small). Douglas, III, 251, 2. O. N. *bragð,* a sudden motion, a quick movement, tricks or sleights in wrestling. O. Sw. *braghþ,* a sudden motion. Norse, Sw. *bragd,* manner of execution, exploit. The fundamental idea in the Sco. and the O. Nh. word is sudden movement. The O. E. *brægd* meant deceit, fraud.

Braith, *adj.* hasty, violent. Wallace, X, 242. O. N. *bráðr,* sudden, hasty, O. Dan. *braadh,* Norse *braad.* Cp. *braahast* (E. Norse), great hurry, O. Sw. *brader, brodher,* hasty, violent, Orm. *bra,* angry. *Brothfall* (Orm), a fit, *broth* (Eng. dial.), in Skeat's list. *Braithful,* violent, sharp.

Braithly, *adv.* violently, suddenly. O. N. *bráðliga,* hastily. Cp. E. Norse *braaleg* adj., and M. Dan. *bradelig.* O. N. *bráðorðr* means "hasty of speech."

Brokit, Brukit, *adj.* streaked, spotted. Burns, 569. O. Sw. *brokoter*, Norse *brokut*, Dan. *broget*, variegated, striped. Cp. *dannebrog*, the Danish flag. Same as Cu. *breukt*. Probably the same with Shetland *brogi*, in "a brogi sky," cloudy. May possibly be Eng. Exists in M. L. G.

Brod, *sb.* a sharp point. Wyntoun, VI, 14, 70. O. N. *broddr*, Norse, Sw. *brodd*, Orm. *brodd*. (See Brate.)

Brod, *vb.* to prick, spur on, incite. C.S. 123; Douglas, III, 3, 20; Dunbar T.M.W. 330. O. N. *brodda*, to prick, to urge. Dan. *brodde* means "to equip with points," a vb. later developed out of the sb.

Bront, *sb.* force, rush, shock. Douglas, I, 90, 20; II, 161, 28. "At the first bront we swept by." See Skeat *brunt*.

Bud, *sb.* a bribe, an offer. Lyndsay, 436, 1616; Dunbar T.M.W. 142. O. N. *bod*, an offer, Norse *bod*, Sw. *bud*, Dan. dial. *bud*, an offer at an auction. Cp. O. E. *friðbote*, a peace-offering, O. N. *frið* + *boð*.

Bught, *sb.* a corner or stall where cows are milked. Ramsay, II, 539. O. N. *bugt*, a bowing, a bight, Norse *bugt*, Dan. *bugt*.

Buller, *vb.* to trickle, bubble. Winyet, II, 62. O. N. *buldra*, Norse *bulrdra*. See E.D.D. cp. Sw. *bullra*, to make an indistinct noise. O. Fr. *bulder*, L. G. *bullern* (see Koolman), Germ. *poltern* all have more the idea of loud noise, clamor, as the Norse word sometimes has. Lyndsay, 226, 95, uses the word in this sense. It may be genuine Eng.

Busk, *vb.* to prepare, dress, adorn, ornament. O. N. *búask* from *búa sik*, to make ready, to ornament. See Wall. Exhibits W. Scand. reflexive ending *sk*. The Gael. *busgainnich*, to dress, to adorn, is a loanword from O. N.

Buskie, *adj.* fond of dress, Jamieson, *busk* sb. dress, decoration. See *busk* vb.

Buith (ŭ), *sb.* booth, shop. Winyet, 1, 23, 2. O. N. *búð*, shop, O. Dan. *both, bodh*. O. Sw. *boð*, Norse *bud*, Sw. *bod*, Dan. dial. *bod*. M. E. *bôþe*, cp. M. L. G. *bode*.

Byng, *vb.* to heap up. Douglas, III, 144, 5. See *bing* sb.

Byrd, *vb.* impers., it behoved. Bruce, VI, 316. O. N. *byrja*, to behove, beseem, pret. *burði*, Norse *byrja* id., pret. *burde*, O. Dan. *böræ*, Sw. *böra*.

Bysning, *adj.* strange, monstrous, terrible, Douglas, I, 29, 7; I, 37, 5; II, 70, 17. M. E. *biseninge*, ill-boding, monstrous, from O. N. *býsna*, to portend, Norse *bisna*, to marvel over.

Bysning, *sb.* a strange person, an unusually unfortunate person. Douglas, I, 2544; I, 339. O. N. *býsna*, to portend, *býsn*, a strange and portentous thing. Norse *bysn*, a prodigy, *bysning*, curiosity. See the adj. Cp. Shetland *sóni-bosni*, O. N. *sjonar-býsn*, a marvel.

Cadye, *adj.* wanton. Lyndsay, LXXXVII, 2567. Also written *cady*, *caidgy*, *caigie*; sometimes means "sportive, cheerful." Dan. *kaad*, merry, lusty, lustful. So Sw. *kåt*, O. N. *katr*, merry, cheerful, Norse *kaat*. Cp. Philotus 5, "the carle caiges," where the same word is used as a vb. to wanton, be wanton.

Caller, *adj.* cool. Fergusson, 73. Very common in modern Sco. diall. O. N. *kaldr*, Norse *kall*, cold. Seems to be a case of the Norse inflexional *r* not disappearing in Sco.

Cangler, a wrangler. Ramsay, II, 482. Norse *kengla*, *kæingla*, *kjæingla*, to quarrel. A Sco. vb. *cangle*, to quarrel, also exists. Cp. O. N. *kangin-yrði*, jeering words, Yorkshire *caingy*, cross, ill-tempered.

Cappit, *vb. pret.* strove. Douglas, II, 154, 21. O. N. *kapp*, contest, zeal, *deila kappi við*, strive with. Norse *kapp* id. *kappa*, reflexive, to race. Dan. *kamp*, O. E. *camp*, *cempam*. The Sco. word exhibits W. Scand. assimilation of *mp* to *pp*, the form *kapp*, however, also existed in O. Sw. and exists in N.Dan. In Cu. a *capper* is one who excels. This is probably the same word. See, however, E.D.

Careing (kçr), *pr. p.* driving, from *care*, *caire*, to drive. Douglas, III, 166, 10; Wallace, IX, 1240. O. N. *köyra*, O. Ic. *keyra*, Norse *køyra*, to drive, ride, O. Ic. *keyrsla*, a driving, Norse *kjørsel*, id. Cp. Shetland *care*, id. Monophthongation in O. Sw. *köra*, Dan. *köre*.

Carl, *sb.* a man, an old man, very frequently with an idea of disrespect. C.S., 144. O. N. *karl*, Norse *kar*, a man, fellow, but *kall*, an old man, with assimilation of *rl* to *ll*. W. Norse *kadl* exhibits the change of *ll* to *dl*. In Dan. and in Sw. dial *karl*. Cu. *carl* means a coarse fellow. Dunbar has the word *wifcarl*, man.

Carlage, *adj.* oldish, decrepit. Irving, 172. O. N. *karl* + *leikr*.

Carling, karling, carline, *sb.* an old woman, a slatternly woman. O. N. *kerling*, an old woman, *karlinna*, a woman. O. Dan. *kærlingh*, O. Sw. *kärling*, Norse *kjæring*, Dan. *kiærling* (pronounced *kælling*), id. Dan. dial. *kerling*. Cp. Gael. *cailliach*. Does not seem to exist in Eng. diall. south of the border.

Carp, karp, *vb.* to talk, converse. Wyntoun, VI, 18, 313. O. N. *karpa*. See Skeat Et.D.

Castings, *sb. pl.* cast off clothes. Dunbar's Complaynt, 43. Deriv. from *cast*. O. N. *kasta*.

Chaft, *sb.* the jaw, also used vulgarly for the mouth. O. N. *kjaptr*, the jaw. Norse *kjæft*, vulgar name for the mouth. O. Sw. *kiäpter*, M. Sw. *käft*, Dan. *kjæft*, M. E. *chaft*.

Chaft-blade, chaff-blade, *sb.* jaw. Mansie Wauch, 41, 20; 76, 23; 147, 28. Cp. Norse *kjæfte-blad*, id. See *chaft*.

Chowk, *sb.* jawbone. Dalr., VIII, 112, 14; Isaiah, L, 6. O. N. *kjálki*, the jawbone, Norse *kjâke*.

Chyngiel, *sb.* gravel. Douglas, III, 302, 30. Norse *singl*, see Skeat, and Wall.

Cled, *pp.* clad, clothed. Wallace, I, 382. O. N. *klæddr*, dressed, from *klæða*. O. E. *clæðan*, from which N. Eng. *clothe*, was borrowed from the Scand. in late O. E. See Kluge P. G.² I., 932

Clag, *sb.* a stain, a flaw. Dalr., VIII, 97, 17. The vowel in O. N. *kleggi* does not correspond. It is rather Dan. *klag*, see *claggit*.

Claggit, *adj.* clagged, literally adhering, sticking, vb. *clag*, to stick. Lindsay, LXXXVII, 2667. Dan. *klæg*, mud, sticky clay, as adj. sticky, cp. Cu.

claggy, adhesive, *clog*, to stick to, O. E. *clæg*, from which N. Eng. *clay*. Possibly from an unpalatalized O. Nhb. *clæg*.

Cleading, *sb.* dress, clothing, A.P.B. 110 cp. Norse *klædning*, Sco. formation, same as clothing in Eng. The Sco. vb. is *cleed*.

Cleckin, *sb.* brood of chickens. Burns, 99, 4. Cp. O. N. *klekking*, chicken, but probably Sco. formation from *cleck*, to hatch, q.v.

Cleg, *sb.* the gadfly, horsefly. Burns, 88, I. O. N. *kleggi*, horsefly, Dan. *kleg*. See Wall.

Clek, *vb.* to hatch. Dunbar, 105; Douglas, II, 198, 3. O. N. *klekja*, O. Sw. *kläkkia*, Norse *klökkja*, *klöttja*, Dan. *klække*, Sw. *kläcka*, id.

Cloff, *sb.* fork, fissure. Montg. F., 60. O. N. *klof*, bifurcation, O. Dan. *klov*, a rift in a tree, O. Sw. *klovi*, id. Norse *klov*, a cleft opening. Cp. Sco. *long-cloved* and Ic. *klof-langr*.

Clour, *vb.* to beat, strike; always used with reference to personal encounters. O. N. *klóra*, to scratch, Norse *klóra* id., *klôr* sb. used with reference to the scratch one gets as the result of a blow. In Sco. *clour* may also mean the blow itself.

Clour, clowre, *sb.* a scratch or swelling after a blow. Fergusson, 120; Philotus, 153; Douglas, I, 6, 4. O. N. *klór*, a scratching. Norse *klôr*. Probably Sco. formation.

Clubbit, *adj.* clubfooted, clumsy. Montg. S., XXVIII; M.P., 13, 30. O. N. *klubba* and *klumba*, Norse *klubba*, Dan., Norse *klump*. Cp. Eng. *clump*. Söderwall gives *klubba, klobba*, probably M. Sw. Cp. N.Dan. *klubbe*. Exhibits assimilation of *mb* to *bb* which is general in W. Scand. Also appears to some extent later in E.Scand. Eng. *club* is Scand. See Skeat.

Clunk, *vb.* to emit a hollow and uninterrupted sound. Jamieson, Ayr. O. N. *klunka*, Norse *klunka*, to emit a gurgling sound. O. Sw. *klunka*, Eng. *clink* shows umlaut.

Clyfft, *sb.* a cleft, a fissure. Wallace, VII, 859. Norse *klyft, kluft*, Ic. *kluft*, Sw. *klyfta*, Dan. *kloft*. See also Skeat under *cleft*, and B.S. *cluft*. The Sco. word like the M. E. exhibits the umlaut which has taken place in some places in Norway and Sweden. Cog, kog, coggie, *sb.* a keg, a wooden vessel of any kind. Ferguson, 13; Burns, 195, 51, 2; 195, 50, 6. O. N. *kaggi*, Norse *kagge*, Dan. Sw. *kagge*, a cask, a barrel. Skeat cites the form *cag* for Eng. diall. The Sco. word preserves more closely the Norse sound, which is not *o*, but *a*. On L. G. cognates see Skeat Et.D.

Costlyk, *adj.* costly, magnificent. Wyntoun, VIII, 28, 76; IX, 18, 66, costlike. O. N. *kostligr*, costly, choice, desirable. O. Sw. *kosteliker*, O. Dan. *kostælic*, N. Dan. *kostelig*, Norse *kosteleg*, costly, magnificent. Deriv. *costlykly*. Wyntoun, VII, 5, 96.

Cour, *vb.* to bow, to croutch. O. N. *kúra*, O. Dan. *kuræ*, O. Sw. *kura*, Norse *kura*, *kurra*, bend down, become quiet, go to rest. Norse *kurr*, adj. silent, *kurrende still*, perfectly quiet, cowered to silence. The fundamental idea in the O. N. word was probably that of "lying quiet." Cp. Shetland *to cur*, to sit down. Isaiah, LVIII, 5: "His head till cower like a seggan flouir."

Cow, *vb.* to overcome, surpass, "beat." O. N. *kúga*, to compel to something, to tyrannize over. Dan *kue*, *underkue*, suppress, oppress, Norse *kua*, press down, also put into subjection. The more general meaning in the modern diall. is "to beat." "To cow a'," in Barrie, to beat everything; *cow'd*, Fergusson 117, terrified.

Craik, *sb.* crow. Burns, 226, 119, 3, and 121, 1. O. N. *kráka*, Norse *kraake*, *krauka*, Dan. *krage*, Shetland *kraga*, crow. See also Wall.

Crave, *vb.* to demand payment of a debt, to dun. A regular Sco. use of the word. O. E. *crafian* is a loanword from Scand. See Kluge P. G.[2] I, 933. Cp. Norse *kreva*, to dun.

Crove, *sb.* hut, cottage. Ramsay, I, 158. O. N. *kró*, a hut, a little cottage (Haldorson), Norse, *kro*, specialized to "wine or ale house." So in Dan.

Cunnand, *adj.* knowing, skilful, dexterous. Wyntoun, VII, 3, 28; *connand*, V, 12, 1243; Douglas, II, 18, 22. O. N. *kunnandi*, knowing, learned, Norse *kunnande*, skilled. Deriv. *cunnandly*, *conandly* (Wallace, I, 248).

Cunnandness, *sb.* skill, knowledge, wisdom. Wyntoun, V, 12, 280; VII, 8, 667. Sb. formation from *cunnand.*

Daggit, *adj. pp.* soaked. Montg. S., 68, 11. O. N. *döggva*, to bedew, *döggottr*, covered with dew, Norse *dogga*, id., Sw. *dagg*, thin, drizzling rain, O. Sw. *dag*, dew, Shetland *dag*, dew, "he's dagen," it is misting. Cp. Cu. *daggy*, misty.

Dapill, *adj.* gray. Douglas, II, 257, 19; Scott 72, 126, "till hair and berd grow dapill." O. N. *depill.* See Skeat.

Dapplet, *adj.* spotted, flecked. Burns, VII, 11. See *dapple* in Skeat Et.D.

Dash, *vb.* to strike. Burns, 210, 872, 8, 7. O. N. *daska*, to strike, sb. *dask*, a strike, Norse *daska*, Dan., Sw. *daska*, M. E. *daschen.* See Bradley's Stratmann.

De, dee, *vb.* to die, M. E. *deyen.* Undoubtedly a Scand. loan-word. Luik (91-93), agreeing with Napier, thinks the word is native from primitive Gmc. **daujan.* I think, however, with Kluge, that if the word had existed in O. E. it would have appeared earlier. See Kluge P. G.[2] I, 933. O. N. *döyja*, Norse *döi*, O. Dan. *döia*, Dan, *dö.* On M. E. *deyen* see Brate.

Degraithit, *pp.* deprived of. Lyndsay, 523, 3935. Formed from the sb. *graith*, possessions, hence *degraith*, to dispossess. Cp. the Eng. parallel. See *graith.*

Dey, dee, *sb.* maid, woman. A.P.B., 151; Ramsay 399. O. N. *dæigja*, a dairy maid, Norse *deigja*, servant, *budeie*, dairy maid, O. Sw. *deghia*, *deijha*, maid, girl, sweetheart, O. Dan. *deije*, mistress, *deijepige*, servant. The Sco. word has nearly always the general sense of "woman."

Ding, *vb.* to drive, strike, beat, overcome. O. N. *dengja*, to hammer, Norse *dengja*, *denge*, to whip, beat, O. Sw. *dängia* id., Sw. *dänge*, O. Dan. *dænge*, M. E. *dingen.* A very common word in Sco., used quite generally as Eng. "beat," in the sense of "surpassing." "To ding a'" = to beat everything. Cp. "to cow a'."

Dirdum, *sb.* tumult, uproar. Douglas, I, 117, 9. O. N. *dýra-dómr,* "doordoom, an ancient tribunal held at the door of the house of the suspected person, which often was followed by uproar and bloodshed" (Small). The word appears in Gael. as *durdan.*

Doif, *adj.* deaf, dull. Irving, 214. See *douff.* For similar parallel forms cp. *gowk* and *goilk; nowt* and *nolt; howk* and *holk; lowp* and *loip; bowdyn* and *boildin,* etc.

Donk, *adj.* damp, moist. Douglas, II, 196, 32; Dunbar, G.T., 97. Cu. *donky.* See Skeat under *dank.* Cp. *donk* sb.

Donk, *sb.* a moist place. Rolland, I, 2. Sw. dial. *dank,* a moist marshy place, small valley. O. N. *dökk,* a pool, Norse *dok,* a valley, Shetland *dek.* Exhibits E. Scand. non-assimilation of *nk* to *kk.*

Donk, *vb.* to moisten. Dunbar, T.M.W., 10, 512. M. E. *donken,* to moisten. See *donk,* adj.

Donnart, *adj.* stupid, stupefied. Mansie Wauch, 96, 29. Norse *daana,* Sw. *dåna,* to faint. For the *r* cp. dumbfoundered, M.W., p. 210, 25. An excrescent *r* appears in a number of words, so in *dynnart,* a variant of the word above, Dunbar, T.M.W. 10. Cp. *daunert,* in stupor, Johnnie Gibb, 56, 44, and *dauner,* to wander aimlessly, Psalms CVII, 40.

Doock, duck. *sb.* a kind of coarse cloth. Jamieson. Probably in this case, as the form of the word indicates, from O. N. *dúkr,* O. Sw. *dúker,* cloth. Cp. Norse *dúk,* Dan. *dug,* Sw. dial. *duk.* Skeat derives the Eng. *duck* from Du. *dock,* but the Sco. word agrees more closely with the Norse.

Dosen, *adj.* stupefied. Burns 220, 107, 2. Cp. Cu. *dozent,* stupefied, and Mansie Wauch, 207, 24, *dozing,* whirling, sprawling. The Norse work *dusen* has the same meaning as *dosen* above. The form *dosynt,* pp. dazed, stunned (Burns), is to be explained from a Sco. vb. *dosen* (not necessarily *dosnen* in Scotland), corresponding to M. E. *dasin,* O. N. *dasa.* See Skeat under *doze.*

Dowff, douf, dolf, *adj.* deaf, dull, melancholy, miserable. Douglas, II, 63, 11; Burns, 44, 4. O. N. *daufr*, deaf, Norse *dauv*, drowsy, dull, *dauva*, make drowsy. See *dowie*.

Dowie, dowy, *adj.* melancholy, dismal. O. N. *doufr*, dead, drowsy. Norse *dauv*, *dau*, id. Cp. Sco. *doolie* and Ir. *doiligh*, mournful, O. N. *daufligr*, dismal.

Dowless, *adj.* careless, worthless. Isaiah, 32, 11. O. N. *duglauss*, Norse *duglaus*, good for nothing, said of a person who has lost all courage or strength, as opposed to *duglegr*, capable. Norse *dugløysa*, weakness, inability. Cp. Dan. *due*, to be able. Germ. *taugen*.

Draik, *vb.* to drown, drench. Lyndsay, 247, 714; *draikit*, Isaiah, I, 22. Apparently from O. N. *drekkja*, to drown, to swamp. The vowel is difficult to explain. The Cu. form *drakt*, drenched, wet, indicates a verb, *drak*. The change in vowel would then be similar to that in *dwall* from O. N. *dvelja*, Eng. *dwell*. Uncertain.

Dram, *sb.* a drink. Fergusson, 40; Mansie Wauch, 9, 9; 90, 2. Norse *dram*, a drink, always used with reference to a strong drink, so in Sco. Dan. *dram*, as much of a strong drink as is taken at one time (Molbeck). O. Sw. *dramb*, drinking in general, carousing. This usage of *dram* is distinctively Scand. and Sco. Cp. Eng. *dram*, Sco. vb. *dram*, to furnish with drinks.

Drawkit, *adj.* drenched. Dunbar 142, 102; Douglas, I, 56, 12; III, 303, 8. See *draik*. The vowel is difficult to explain. Absence of *n* before the *k* proves that it is either a Scand. loanword direct, or a Sco. formation from one. There is no Scand. word from which *drawkit* could come. It may be a Sco. formation from *draik*. For change of *ai* to *aw* cp. *agent* and *awgent*; *various* and *vawrious*, in Aberdeen dial. The M. Dan. *drockne*, N. Norse *drokna*, would hardly account for *aw* in *drawkit*.

Drook, to drench, to drown. Isaiah, XVI, 9; LV, 10; Psalms, VI, 6. Cannot come from O. N. *drekkja*. Probably from O. N. *drukna*, to drown, Norse *drukna*, O. Dan. *dronkne*, by lengthening of the vowel. Cp. Cu.

drookt, severely wet. The following infinitive forms also occur, *draik*, *drowk*, *drawk*.

Droukit, *adj.* drenched. Fergusson, 40. See *drook*.

Drucken, druken, *adj.* drunken, addicted to drink. O. N., Norse *drukken*, pp. of *drikka*, to drink. Early E. Scand. has the unassimilated form. Cp. O. Dan. *dronkne*, *drone*. Later Dan. *drougne*, *drocken*. Early Sw. *drokken*.

Duddy, *adj.* ragged. Fergusson, 146; Burns, 68, 48. See *duds*. Cp. Cu. *duddy fuddiel*, a ragged fellow.

Duds, *sb. pl.* rags, clothes, O. N. *dudi*, "vestes plumatae" (Haldorson), *duda* (*duða*), to wrap up heavily, to swaddle. Gael. *dud*, rag, is a loan-word from O. N. It is possible that the word may have come into Lowland Sco. by way of Gael.

Egg, *vb.* to urge on, to incite. O. N. *eggja*, goad, incite, Norse *egga*, Dan. *egge*, id. The word is general Gmc., but this specific sense is Scand. Cp. O. Fr. *eggia*, to quarrel, to fight. M. L. G. *eggen*, to cut, to sharpen a sword.

Egging, *sb.* excitement, urging. Bruce, IV, 539. See *egg*.

Eident, ydan, ythand, *adj.* diligent. Dalr., I, 233, 35; Fergusson, 94; Douglas, I, 86, 17. O. N. *iðinn*, assiduous, diligent, *iðja*, to be active. Norse *idn*, activity, industry. Cp. Dan. *id*, *idelig*.

Elding, *sb.* fuel. Dalr., I, 10, 8. O. N. *elding*, firing, fuel. Norse *elding*, id. Cu. *eldin*. From O. N. *eldr*, fire. Cp. Shetland *eld*, fire. See N.E.D.

Eldnyng, *sb.* passion, also jealousy. Dunbar, 36, 204; 119, 126, literally "firing up." O. N. *eldr*, fire. Cp. Sw. *elding*.

Encrely, ynkirly, *adv.* especially, particularly. Bruce, I, 92; I, 301; X, 287. O. N. *einkarlegr*, O. Dan. *enkorlig*, O. Sw. *enkorlika*, adj. adv. special, especially. Cp. Norse *einkeleg*, unusual, extraordinary. See B-S and Skeat's glossary to Barbour's Bruce.

End, *sb.* breath. Sat. P., 42, 63. See *aynd*.

End, *vb.* to breathe upon. Dalr., I, 29, 6. O. N. *anda*, Norse *anda*, breathe, M. E. *anden*.

Erd, *vb.* to bury. Dunbar, F., 372; Douglas, II, 266, 10; Bruce, XX, 291. O. N. *jarða*, to bury, O. Sw. *iorþa*. O. E. *eardian* meant "to dwell, inhabit." See further Wall. A case of borrowed meaning, the form is Eng.

Erding, *sb.* burial. Bruce, IV, 255; XIX, 86. See *erd* vb.

Espyne, *sb.* a long boat. Bruce, XVII, 719. O. N. *espingr*, a ship's boat, Sw. *esping*.

Ettil, etil, *sb.* aim, design. Douglas, II, 249, 13; II, 254. See *ettil* vb.

Etlyng, *sb.* aim, endeavor, intention. Bruce, II, 22; I, 587; R.R., 1906. Probably a deriv. from *ettle*, see below, but cp. O. N. *etlun*, design, plan, intention.

Ettle, ettil, *vb.* to intend, aim at, attempt. O. N. *ætla*, intend, O. Dan. *ætlæ*, ponder over, Norse *etla*, intend, determine, or get ready to do a thing. Cu. *ettle*, York, *attle*. In Isaiah, LIX, colophon, *ettle* signifies "means, have the meaning."

Falow, *vb.* to match, compare. R. R., 3510. Also the regular form of the sb. in Sco., O. N. *félagr*. See Skeat, B-S under *fçlaȝe*. The Sco. vowel is long as in O. N. and M. E. The tendency in Sco. is toward *a* in a great many words that have *e* in Eng. Cp. Aberdeen *wast* for *west*; *laft* for *left*; *stap* for *step*; *sattlit* for *settled*, S. Sco. *wat* for *wet*. Similar unfronting of the vowel is seen in *prenciple*, *reddance*, *enterdick*.

Fang, *vb.* to catch, seize. O. N. *fanga*, to fetch, capture. Norse *fanga*, Dan. *fange*. This word in Northern England and Scotland is to be regarded as a Scand. loan-word. The word *fangast*, a marriageable maid, cited by Wall, proves this. Literally the word means something caught (cp. Norse *fangst*). This meaning could not possibly have arisen out of the O. E. word, but is explained by the Norse use of it and the peculiar Norse custom, cp. *fanga kǫnu*, to wed a woman, *kvan-fang*, marriage, *fangs-tíð*, wedding-season, Norse *bryllöp* < *brudlaup*, the "bride-run."

Wall suggests that it may come from the root of O. E. pp. *gefangen*. Its presence in S.Eng. diall. in the meaning "to struggle, to bind," may be explained in this way.

Farandness, *sb.* comeliness, handsomeness. R.R., 1931. See *farrand*. Cp. *cunnandness*, from pr. p. *cunnand*.

Farrand, *adj.* appearing, generally well-appearing, handsome, e.g., *a seemly farrand person*. The word frequently means "fitting, proper," O. N. *fara*, to suit, to fit, a secondary sense of *fara*, to go.

Feir, fer, *adj.* sound, unharmed. O. N. *færr*, safe, well, in proper condition, originally applied to a way that was in proper condition or a sea that was safe, e.g., *Petlandsfjörðr var eigi færr*, the Pentland Firth was not safe, could not be crossed. Norse *før* also has this same meaning, also means "handy, skillful," finally "strong, well-built." Dan., Sw. *för*, able. So in Dunbar, 258, 51. Sometimes spelled *fier*.

Fell, *sb.* mountain. O. N. *fjald*, Norse *fjell*. See Wall.

Fillok, *sb.* a giddy young woman. Douglas, III, 143, 10; Lyndsay, 87, 2654. Diminutive of *filly*, q.v.

Filly, *sb.* a chattering, gossipy young woman. Ramsay, II, 328. Sco. usage. See Skeat under *filly*, O. N. *fylja*.

Firth, *sb.* a bay, arm of the sea. O. N. *fjörðr*, O. Sw. *fjördher*. See Skeat.

Flake, *sb.* a hurdle. Douglas, IV, 14, 10. O. N. *flaki*, a hurdle, or shield wicker-work. Norse *flake*, Sw. *flake* and O. Sw. *flaki*. Cu. *flaks*, pieces of turf, is probably the same. Cp. Norse *flake*, in *kote-flake*.

Flat, *adj.* dull, spiritless. Rolland, Prol. 16. O. N. *flat*, Norse *flat*, ashamed, disappointed, *fara flatt fyrir einem*, to fare ill, be worsted, O. Dan. *flad*, weak.

Fleckerit, *pp. adj.* spotted. Gol. and Gaw., 475. O. N. *flekkr*, a spot, *flekkóttr*, spotted. The *r* in the Sco. word is frequentative, not the inflexional ending of the O. N. See also Skeat under *fleck*.

Flegger, *sb.* a flatterer. Dunbar, F., 242. Dan. dial. *flægger*, false, *flægre*, to flatter.

Flingin tree, *sb.* a piece of timber hung by way of partition between two horses in a stable (Wagner), Burns, 32, 23. O. N. *flengja*, Norse *flenga*, *flengja*, to fling, to sling. Sw. *flänga*, O. Ic. *flengja*, to whip up, to cause to hurry, to ride furiously. The Norse and the Dan., like the English, do not have the primary meaning seen in O. Ic. and N.Sw. See further Skeat.

Flit, *vb.* to move, change abode. O. N. *flyttja*, Norse *flytta*, O. Dan. *flyttæ*, O. Sw. *flyttia*, to move, M. E. *flytten*. The O. N. *flyttja* meant "to migrate," as also the M. E. word, otherwise the usage is the same in all the Scand. languages. Sco. *flit* is to be derived from O. N. not from Sw.

Flyre, *vb.* to grin, leer, whimper, look surly. Montg. F., 188. Dunbar, T.M.W., 114. O. N., *flira*, Norse *flira*, smile at, leer, laugh, Dan. *flire* to leer, M. E. *fliren*. The three words *flina*, *flira* and *flisa* in Scand. mean the same. Cu. *fliar*, to laugh heartily. See also Wall.

Flytting, *sb.* furniture, moveable goods. Wyntoun, VIII, 38, 50. In Wallace simply in the sense of removal. O. N. *flutning*, transport, carriage of goods. The Sco. word is probably a deriv. from *flyt*, as indicated also by the umlauted vowel.

Forelders, *sb. pl.* parents. Gau. 15, 2. Dan. *forældre*, Sw. *föräldrar*, Norse *foreldre*, parents. In the sense "ancestors" the word is general Gmc, but the above use is specifically Scand. In Sco. the word usually has the general sense. Gau has Dan. elements that are not to be found in other Sco. works.

Forjeskit, *adj.* jaded, fatigued. Burns, 44, 29. Dan. *jask* adj., *jaske* vb. to rumple, put in disorder, *jask*, a rag, *jasket*, *hjasket* left in disordered condition. Dan. dial. *jasked*, clumsy, homely. Sw. dial. *jaska*, to walk slovenly and as if tired, *jasked*, adj. in bad condition. R.L. Stevenson in "The Blast" uses *forjaskit* in the sense of "jaded." The prefix *for* may be either Eng. or Dan.

Forloppin, *adj.* renegade. Sat., p. 44, 243. The pp. of *loup*, to leap, to run, with intensive prefix *for*. See *loup*. Cp. the Norse *forloppen* from *læupa*, used precisely in the same way, and the Dan. dial. *loben. Forloppin* as sb., Dunbar, 139. See also *loppert.*

Fors, *sb.* a stream. O. N. *fors*, N.Ic. and Norse *foss*, Dan., Sw. *foss*, stream, waterfall, O. N. *forsa*, to foam, spout. The word is very common in Norway, not so common in Sweden and Denmark.

Forth, *sb.* Dunbar, 316, 63. Same as *firth.*

Fra, Frae, *prep.* and *conj.* from, since. Aberdeen form *fae*. O. N. *frá*, from, Dan. *fra*, Norse *fra*, Sw. *frå*. Deriv. from "from," according to Wall, by analogy of *o'*, etc. I do not believe so. It is first found in Scand. settlements and is confined to them. Besides *m* would not be likely to fall out. The case is quite different with *f* and *n* in "of" and "in" when before "the." Furthermore, the conjunctive use of *fra* as in Sco. is Norse.

Frecklit, freckled, *adj.* flecked, spotted, differing slightly from the Eng. use. Douglas, II, 216, 5; Mansie Wauch, 18, 5, "freckled corn." O. N. *freknur.* See Kluge and Lutz, and Skeat. In M.W. above: "The horn-spoons green and black freckled."

Frend, *sb.* relation, relative. Wyntoun, VII, 10, 354. O. N. *frændi*, kinsman, O. Dan. *frændi*, Norse *frænde*, Sw. *frände*, id. O. E. *frĕond*, O. H.G. *friunt*, O. Fr. *friond, friund*, M. L. G. *vrint*, "friend." Cp. the Sco. proverb: "Friends agree best at a distance," relations agree best when there is no interference of interests, Jamieson.

Frestin, *vb.* to tempt, taunt, also to try. Gol. and Gaw., 902, 911; Ramsay, I, 271. O. N. *fræista*, to tempt, Norse *freista, frista*, to tempt, try, O. Sw. *fresta*, Dan. *friste*, Sw. dial. *freista*, to attempt, O. E. *frâsian.*

Ganand, *adj.* fitting, proper. Dunbar, 294; Douglas, II, 24, 19. Pr. p. of *gane.* Cp. Eng. fitting. See *gane.*

Gane, *vb.* to be suitable. L.L., 991; Rolland, II, 135. O. N. *gegna*, to suit, to satisfy, from *gegn.* O. Sw. *gen*, same root in Germ. *begegnen.* See further Kluge. Entirely different from *gane*, to profit.

Gane, *vb.* to profit. L.L., 131; R.R., 1873. O. N. *gagne*, to help, be of use, *gagn*, use, profit, Norse *gagna*, id., O. Sw. *gaghna*, to profit, Dan. *gavne*.

Gane, *sb.* the mouth and throat. Douglas, III, 168, 26. Cannot come from O. E. *gin*, O. N. *gin*, mouth, because of the quality of the vowel, is, however, Norse *gan*, *gane*, the throat, the mouth and throat, Sw. *gan*, *gap*, the inside of the mouth.

Gait, gate, gat, *sb.* road, way, manner. O. N. *gata*, O. Dan. *gatæ*, M. E. *gâte*. See Wall. Cp. Northern Eng. "to gang i' that rwoad," to continue in that manner.

Garth, gairth, *sb.* the yard, the house with the enclosure, dwelling. O. N. *garðr*, a yard, the court and premises, O. Sw. *garþer*, *gardh*, the homeplace, Dan. *gaard*, M. E. *garth*, and *yeard* from O. E. *geard*, Cu. *garth*, Shetland *gard*. Is in form more specifically Norse than Dan. Occurs in a number of place-names in South Scotland, especially Dumfries. See I, § 3.

Gatefarrin, *adj.* wayfaring, in the sense of fit to travel, in suitable apparel for travel. Johnnie Gibb, 12, 35. Wall distinguishes rightly between the O. N. and the Eng. use of the word *fare*. This Scand. use of the word is confined to Norway and Iceland, and is, at any rate in the later period, more characteristic of Icelandic than Norse. Cp. a similar use of the word *sitta*, in Norse, to look well, said of clothes that look well on a person. Not quite the same.

Gawky, *adj.* foolish. Burns, 78, 60. From *gowk*. Cp. *gawkish*.

Gedde, *sb.* a pike (fish). Bruce, II, 576; Sat. P. I, 53, 9. O. N. *gedda*, the pike, Dan. *gjedde*, Sw. *gädda*. Not in M. E., except in Sco. works, and does not seem to exist in Eng. diall.

Gemsal, yemseill, yhemsale, *sb.* concealment, secrecy. Bruce, XX, 231; Wyntoun, VIII, 19, 206; VIII, 36, 84. O. N. *göymsla*, O. Ic. *geymsla*, Norse *gøymsla*, *gøymsel*, concealment. Dano-Norse *gjemsel*. The ending *sal* is distinctively Scand. Cp. *trængsel*, misery; *længsel*, longing; *hørsel*, hearing; *pinsel*, torture; *trudsel*, threat; *opførsel*, conduct; Sco. *tynsell, hansell*, etc.

Genȝeld, *sb.* reward, recompense. Douglas, II, 100, 12; II, 111, 17; Scott, 59, 62. O. N. *gegn-gjald*, reward, O. Dan. *gengæld, giengiald* id., *giengielde*, to reward, Norse *gjengjæld. Gen* is the same as the *gegn* in *gegna*, to suit,-ȝeld can be either Scand. or Eng. The palatal *g* is also Scand. in this word. The compound *genȝeld* is Scand. In Sco. also spelled *ganȝeld, gaynȝeild*.

Ger, gar, *vb.* to make, cause, force. O. N. *gera* (Cl. and V.). O. Dan. *göræ*, Sw. *göra*, Norse *gjera*, to do, to make. O. Nh. *görva. Gar* is the modern form which exhibits regular Sco. change of *er* to *ar*. Cp. *serk, sark; werk, wark*.

Gestnyng, *sb.* hospitality. Douglas, III, 315, 8. O. N. *gistning*, a passing the night as a guest at a place, *gista*, vb. to spend the night with one, *gestr*, guest. O. Dan. *gæstning*, O. Sw. *gästning, gistning*.

Glete, gleit, *vb.* to glitter. Douglas, I, 33; II, 88, 16; Montg. C. and S., 1288; Dunbar, G.T., 66. O. N. *glita*, to glitter, Dan. *glitte*. Cp. Shetland *glid*, a glittering object. O. E. *glitnian* > M. E. *glitenien*, as O. E. *glisnian* > M. E. *glistnian*, N. Eng. *glisten*. The M. E. *glitenian* (N.Eng. **glitten*) was replaced by the Scand. *glitter*.

Gleit, *sb.* literally "anything shining," used in Palace of Honour, II, 8, for polish of speech. See the vb.

Gley, *sb.* a look, glance, stare. Mansie Wauch, 85, 10; 117, 37. See Wall, *gley*, to squint, B-S. *glien*. Cp. Sw. dial. *glia*.

Gleg, *adj.* sharp. See Wall, deriv. *glegly*, quickly.

Glitterit, *adj.* full of glitter. Dunbar, T.M.W., 30. See *glitter* in Skeat.

Gowk, *sb.* a fool. O. N. *gaukr*, Norse *gæuk*, O. Sw. *göker*, Dan. *gjög*. In Sco. very frequently spelled *goilk, golk*. Cu. *April-gowk*, April fool.

Gowl, *vb.* to scream, yell. O. N. *gaula*, Norse *gæula*, to yell, to scream. Shetland *gjol, gol*, to howl, seems to be the same word, but the palatal before *o* is strange. Cp. Sco. *gowle*.

Gowlynge, *sb.* screaming, howling. R.R. 823, pr. p. of *gowl.* Cp. O. N. *gaulan,* Norse *gæuling,* sb. screaming.

Graip, *sb.* a dung-fork. Burns, 38, 1, 2. Johnnie Gibb, 102, 18; 214, 21. Norse *græip,* id., Dan. *greb,* a three-pronged fork.

Graith, *adj.* ready, direct. Bruce, IV, 759; Wallace, V, 76. O. N. *græiðr,* ready, Norse *greid,* simple, clear, ready. Deriv. *graithly,* directly, Gol. and Gau. 54. Cp. Yorkshire *graidly,* proper.

Graith, *vb.* make ready, dress, furnish, equip. C.S., 39; R.R., 424; Psalms XVIII, 32. O. N. *græiða,* to disentangle, set in order, make ready. Norse *greide,* to dress (the hair). Cu. *graitht,* dressed.

Grane, *sb.* twig, branch. Douglas, II, 10, 27; Dunbar, 76. O. N. *græin,* Norse *grein,* Dan. *gren,* O. Sw. *gren,* branch. The Dan. and Sw. forms show monophthongation. The Sco. word agrees best with the Norse.

Granit, *adj.* forked. Douglas, II, 133, 4. O. N. *græina,* to branch, divide into branches, separate. Norse *græina,* Sw., Dan. *grena,* id., O. Sw. *grenadh,* adj. forked, Cu. *grainet.*

Grayth, graith, *sb.* equipment, possessions. Dunbar, 229; Lyndsay, 154, 4753; Burns, 23, 18. O. N. *græiða,* means "tools, possessions," originally "order." Cp. the vb. In Douglas, III, 3, 25, *graith* means "preparation."

Graithly, *adv.* directly, speedily. Bruce, XIX, 708; X, 205. O. N. *græiðliga,* readily, promptly.

Grith, *sb.* peace, truce. Wallace, X, 884. O. N., O. Dan. *grið,* truce, protection, peace. O. Sw. *grið, gruð.* Occurs very often in the parts of the A-S. Chronicle dealing with the wars with the Danes, for the first time in 1002. "*Frið and grið,*" meant "truce," or "peace and protection." See Steenstrup's discussion of these words, pp. 245-250.

Grouf, on growfe, *adj.* prone, on one's face. Douglas, IV, 20, 24; Dunbar, 136, 12. O. N. *á grúfu,* grovelling. Norse *aa gruva,* id., O. Sw. *a gruvo.* Sw. diall. *gruva, å gruv,* Dan. *paa gru.*

Grys, gryce, *sb.* a pig. Douglas, II, 143, 14; Lyndsay, 218, 300; Montg., F., 88. O. N. *griss,* a young pig, swine, O. Dan. *gris,* Norse *gris.*

Gukk, *vb.* to act the fool. Dunbar, F., 497. Probably to be derived from *gowk*, sb. a fool. It cannot very well come from *geck*, to jest, the vowels do not correspond. In Poet. R., 108, 5, *gukit* means "foolish, giddy."

Gyll, *sb.* cleft, glen, ravine. Douglas, III, 148, 2; Sat. P., 12, 71. O. N. *gil*, a narrow glen with a stream at the bottom, Norse *gil*, *gyl*, a mountain ravine. Cp. Cu. *gill*, *ghyll*.

Gylmyr, *sb.* a ewe in her second year. C.S., 66. O. N. *gymbr*, a ewe lamb a year old, also *gymbr-lamb*, Norse *gymber*, Dan. *gimber*, M. E. *gimbir*, *gimbyr*, Cu. *gimmer*. In northwestern England and Scotland assimilation of *mb* to *mm* took place. Our word has excrescent *l*, cp. *chalmer*, not uncommon.

Gyrth, *sb.* a sanctuary, protection. Bruce, IV, 47; II, 44; C.S., 115. O. N. *grið*, a sanctuary, a truce. O. Sw. *grið*, *gruð*, M. Norse *gred*, protection. Cu. *gurth*, cp. *grith*.

Gyrth *sb.* a hoop for a barrel, the barrel. R.R., 27, 81. O. N. *gjörð*, a girdle, a hoop, Dan. *gjord*, Norse *gjord*, *gjaar*, *gjoir*, hoop, girdle, O. E. form *gyrd*. Cp. O. N. *girða*, to gird, and *girði*, wood for making hoops.

Gyrthyn, *sb.* saddle-strap, saddle-band. Wyntoun, VIII, 36, 64. O. N. *gjörð*. See Skeat, *girth*. Our word is not nominative pl. as the editor of Wyntoun takes it, but is the singular originally pr. p. of *girth*, to gird, to strap. In Poet. R. 113, occurs the form *girthing*. Cp. Cu. *girting*, *girtings*.

Hailse, *vb.* to greet, salute. Bruce, II, 153; C.S., 141. O. N. *helsa*, older *hæilsa*, to hailsay one, to greet, O. Sw. *helsa*, Dan. *hilse*, Norse *helsa*, id., M. E. *hailsen*. This word is entirely different from O. E. *healsian*, which is *heals + ian* and meant "beseech, implore," literally "embrace." The form of this was *halsian* in O. Nhb., from which Sco. *hawse*, to embrace.

Hailsing, halsing, *sb.* a salute, greeting. Douglas, II, 243, 31; Dunbar "Freires of Berwick" 57; Rosw. and Lill. 589. O. N., O. Sw., Norse *helsa*, see above; Norse *helsing,* Dan. *hilsning,* a greeting. *Hailsing* formed direct from the vb. *hailse.*

Haine, *vb.* to protect, save. Fergusson, 171; Psalms LXXVIII, 50; LXXX, 19; *we're hain'd,* we are saved. O. N. *hegna,* to hedge in, protect, *hegnaðr,* defence, Norse *hegna,* Dan. *hegne,* O. Sw. *häghna,* to hedge in for the sake of protecting. Cu. *hain.*

Hained, *pp. adj.* sheltered, secluded, cp. *a hained rig,* Burns, 8, 1. In modern usage very frequently means "saved up, hoarded," so *hained gear,* hoarded money. See *haine* above.

Hainin' tower, *sb.* fortress. Psalms XVIII, 2; XXXI, 2; LXII, 7. See *hain.*

Haling (hçling), *pr. p.* pouring down. Douglas, II, 47, 31. O. N. *hella,* to pour out water, *helling,* sb. pouring. See Wall under *hell.* We should expect a short vowel as generally in Eng. diall. The form *hale,* however, occurs in Yorkshire too. Both are from O. N. *hella.* There is no Scand. or L. G. word with original *a* to explain *hale,* but cp. the two words *dwell* and *wail,* to choose. *Dwell* from O. N. *dvelja,* preserves both quality and quantity of the original vowel. The Sco. form is, however, *dwall.* Here the vowel has been opened according to Sco. tendency of changing *e* to *a* before liquids, cp. *félag > falow,* also frequently before other consonants. Cp. the same tendency in certain dialects in America, so *tăll* or even *tǣl* for *tell,* *băll* for *bell,* *wăll* for *well,* etc. If *e* before *l* in *hell,* to pour, was changed to *a,* as *e* in *dwell,* and later lengthened, we would have the form *hǣl* out of which *hale* would be regularly developed, and so a double development from the same word, *hell* and *hale.* *Wail,* to choose, might be explained in the same way from O. N. vb. *velja.* *Well* would be the regular form, but this is not found. The O. N. *val,* choice, is, however, sufficient to explain *wail.*

Hame-Sucken, *sb.* the crime of assaulting a person within his own house. O. N. *hæim-sókn,* O. Dan. *hem-sokn,* an attack on one's house. O. Sw. *hem-sokn,* O. E. *hamsocn,* E. *ham-socne.* See Steenstrup, pp. 348-349. The word seems to have come into Eng. during the time of the

Danes in England, though both elements are Eng. as well as Scand. See Kluge, P. G.² I, 933.

Hammald, *adj.* domestic. Douglas, II, 26, 7. O. N. *heimoll, heimill*, domestic, O. Sw. *hemoll*, Norse *heimholt*. Excrescent *d* after *l* quite common in Scand. and appears in Sco. in a few words. See *fald*.

Hank, *sb.* thread as it comes from the measuring reel, a coil of thread. Burns, 584. See Skeat. Cu. *hankle*, to entangle, is probably the same word.

Hansel, *sb.* gift. O. N. *handsal*. Bruce, V, 120, *hansell* used ironically means "defeat." See Skeat.

Harn, *sb.* brain. O. N. *hjarni*, brain, O. Dan. *hiʒrnć*, Norse *hjarne*, Dan. *hjerne*, O. Sw. *hiärne, härne*.

Harsk, *adj.* harsh, cruel. Wyntoun, IX, 1, 27; Douglas, II, 208, 17. O. N. **harsk*, bitter, as proved by Shetland, *ask, hask, hosk*, and Norse *hersk*. Cp. Dan. *harsk*. O. Ic. *herstr*, bitter, hard, severe, is probably the same word, *st* to *sk*. Cp. Cu. *hask weather*, dry weather. Shetland, *hoski wadder*, dry and windy weather (Jakobson, p. 68). Dan. dial. *harsk*, bitter, dry. For dropping of *r*, as in the Shetland form, cp. *kask*, from *karsk*, in "Havelok," cited in Skeat's list.

Harskness, *sb.* harshness. Dunbar, 104, 19. See *harsk*.

Harth, *adj.* hard. Dunbar, F., 181; O. N. *harðr*, Norse *har(d)*, Dan. *haar(d)*, hard.

Haugh, *sb.* a hill, a knoll. O. N. *haugr*, a hill, Norse *haug*, Old Gutnic *haugr*, Cu. *howe*. The O. Sw. *högher*, O. Dan. *hög, höw*, Dan. *höi*, Shetland *hjog, hög*, show later monophthongation. Cp. M. E. *houʒ, hogh*.

Haver-meal, *sb.* oat-meal. Burns, 187, 32, 1. Cp. Norse, *havremjöl*, O. N. *hafrmjöl*, Dan. *havre meel*. The first element of the compound is used especially in Scand. settlements in England and is probably due to Scand. influence. An O. S. *hafore* exists, but if our word is native, it ought to be distributed in South Eng. diall. as well. The second element of the compound may be Eng.

Haynd, *sb.* Douglas, III, 119, 6. See *aynd*.

Heid, *sb.* brightness. Rolland, I, 122. O. N. *hæið*, brightness of the sky, *hæið ok sólskin*, brightness and sunshine, *hæiða*, to brighten, *hæiðbjartr*, serene. Cp. *heiðs-há-rann*, the high hall of brightness, an O. poetical name for heaven. The Norse adj. *heid*, bright, like the Sco. word, shows change of *ð* to *d*.

Hendir, *adj.* past, bygone. Bruce, 10, 551. Dunbar's poem, *This hendir Night*. O. N. *endr*, formerly. Cp. *ender-day* in Skeat's list.

Hething, *sb.* scorn, mockery. Wyntoun, IX, 10, 92; Wallace, V, 739; Douglas, II, 209, 7. O. N. *háðing*, sb. scoffing, scorn, *háða*, to scoff, to mock, Norse, *hæding*, scorn, mockery, O. Sw. *hädha*, *hödha*.

Hing, *vb.* to hang. Lindsay, 527, 4033; Gol. and Gaw., 438; Psalms LXIX, 6. Same as Cu. *hing*, for which see Wall.

Hooli, hulie, *adj.* quiet, slow, leisurely, careful. Dalr., I, 149, 27; A.P.B., 41; Fergusson, 54. O. N., *hógligr*, easy, gentle, *hógleiki*, meekness, *hóglifi*, a quiet life, *hóglyndr*, good-natured.

Hugsum, *adj.* horrible. Wyntoun, VII, 5, 176. See *ug*, to fear.

Husband, *sb.* a small farmer. Bruce, X, 387; VII, 151. O. N. *hús-bondi*, a house-master. See Skeat. For full discussion of this word as well as *bonde*, see Steenstrup, 97-100.

Ill, *adj.* evil, wicked. Bruce, III, 10. O. N. *illr*, adj. bad, Norse *ill*, *idl*, cross, angry, Dan. *ilde*, adv. badly. As an adv. common in M. E. The adj. use of it more specifically Sco. as in Norse. See Skeat.

Irke, *vb.* to weary, to suffer. Dunbar, F., 429; R.R., 456; L.L., 2709. O. N. *yrkja*, to work, take effect, O. Sw. *yrkja*, O. Dan. *yrki* (Schlyter), Sw. *yrke*, to urge, enforce, Norse *orka*, be able, always used in the sense of "barely being able to," or, with the negative, "not being able to." Ramsay uses the word in the sense of "being vexed."

Irke, *adj.* weary, lazy. Dunbar, 270, 36; R.R., 3570. See *irke*, vb. *Irkit*, pp. adj. tired, Montg., M.P., 521.

Irking, *sb.* delay. Winyet, II, 76; I. Deriv. from *irke*, vb.

Ithandly, ythandly, ydanlie, *adv.* busily, assiduously. Dalr., II, 36, 12; R.R., 36, 95. O. N. *iðinn*, busy. See *eident*.

Karping, carping, *sb.* speech, address. Wyntoun, VIII, 18, 85; VIII, 18, 189; IX, 9, 34. See *carp*.

Keik, kek, *vb.* to peep, to pry. O. N. *kíkja*, to pry, Norse *kika*. Undoubtedly a Scand. loan-word, *i>ei* as in *gleit, gley*.

Kendle, kendill, kennle, *vb.* to kindle. Lyndsay, 161, 4970; Gol. and Gaw., 1221; Rolland, I, 609. O. N. *kendill, kynda*, M. E. *kindlen*. See Brate.

Kilt, *vb.* to tuck up, O. N. *kelta, kjalta*, O. Dan. *kiltæ*, the lap, Dan., Norse *kilte*, to tuck up, O. Sw. *kilta*, sb. For discussion of this word see Skeat.

Kist, kyst, *sb.* chest, box. O. N. *kista*, Norse, Dan. *kiste*, a chest. O. E. *cest* would have given *kest*, or *chest*. See also Curtis, § 392. The tendency in Sco. is to change *i* to *e* before *st*, not *e* to *i*. Cp. *restit, gestning*.

Kittling, kittlen, *sb.* kitten. Burns, 38, 2, 3; Mansie Wauch, 23, 19; 210, 10. O. N. *ketlingr*, diminutive of *ketta*, she-cat, Norse *kjetling*. Cp. Cu. *kitlin*. The same diminutive formation appears in Dan. *kylling*, older *kykling*, Norse *kjukling*, a chicken.

Knuse, knoose, *vb.* to bruise, to press down with the knees, to beat, also to knead. Ramsay, I, 236. See Jamieson for secondary meanings. O. N. *knusa*, to bruise, to beat, Norse *knusa*, Dan. *knuse*, crush, O. Sw. *knosa, knusa*, crush, press tight, beat. Cp. Goth. *knusian*. O. E. *cnysian*, shows umlaut.

Kow, *sb.* a fright, terror. Winyet, I, 107, 12. O. N. *kúga*, to cow. See *cow*, vb.

Lack, *vb.* to belittle, blame, reproach, despise. Mont., M.P., 43, 17; R.R., 3242; 3517; Gau., 17, 25. O. N. *hlakka*, to look down upon, O. Dan. *lakke*, to slander, O. Sw. *belacka*, id. See *lak*, sb.

Laiching, *sb.* sport, play. R.R., 647. From Sco. vb. *laike*, to play, O. N. *læika*. See *lak*.

Laif, lave, *sb.* the rest. O. N. *læif*, a leaving, pl. *læifar*, remnants, Norse *leiv*, id., *løyva*, to leave. Cannot come from O. E. *lâf.* See § 20.

Laigh, *adj.* low. Ramsay, II, 20; Mansie Wauch, 106, 23. Same as Eng. *low*, from O. N. *lágr*, O. Sw. *lagher*, O. Dan. *lagh, lag*, low. In Eng., O. N. *ag* > *ǫw* > *ow*. In Scotland *ag* > *aw*, did not become *ow* later. So the regular Sco. form is *law*, or, with guttural, *lawch*. In *laigh*, however, *a* has developed as *a* would when not before *g* or *h*. The form *logh* also occurs. In Dunbar occur *low, law, laich*, and *loigh*.

Laigh, *vb.* to bend down, to kneel. Psalms XCV, 6. See *laigh*, adj.

Laike, *sb.* the stake for which one plays. Montg., C., I, 109. O. N. *læikr*, a play, Norse *leik*, O. Dan. *legh*. Also means play in Sco., but the transferred meaning is common. It cannot come from O. E. *lâc*. The *e*-vowel in Cu., Westm., and S. Scotland proves an original *æi*-diphthong. See Part I, § 16.

Lairet, *adj.* bemired. Psalms LXIX, 2. Norse *læir*, clay. Dan. dial. *ler*, O. Sw. *leer, ler*, id., Eng. dial. *lair*. See Wall. Jamieson gives *lair*, vb. to stick in the mire, *lair*, sb. a bog, *lairy*, adj. boggy.

Lairing, *sb.* gutter, deep mud. Burns, 10, 11. O. N. *læir*, clay. Same as Yorkshire *lyring*, for which see Wall. *Lyring* seems to show original E. Scan. monophthongation of *æi* to *e*.

Lait, *sb.* manner, trick. R.R., 273, 25, 36. O. N., Ic. *lát*, manners, *skipta lítum ok látum*, change shape and manners. O. Sw. *lat*, manner, way of proceeding. Cp. O. N. *láta-læti*, dissimulation, *látbragð*, gestures, and Dan. *lade*, to dissimulate, pretend. Norse *lata*, id. Probably related to O. N. *lát.*

Layking, *sb.* jousting, a tournament. Wyntoun, VIII, 35. See *laik*.

Lak, *sb.* a plaything. Wallace, VIII, 1410. Norse *leik*, a game, *leiker* (pl.), games, toys. Sw. dial. *leika*, a doll, a play sister. Cp. Cu. *lakin*, a child's toy.

Lak, *sb.* contempt, reproach, disgrace. Rolland, I, 455; Rosw. and Lill., 784; R.R., 3092. O. N. *lakr*, defective, O. Dan. *lak*, fault, deficiency. Sw.

lack, fault, slander. O. Sw. *lakkare*, a slanderer. Cp. Dan. *lakkeskrift*, a satirical piece. See *lack*, vb.

Leister, *sb.* a three-pronged salmon spear. Burns, 16, 1. Dumfries and Ayr., any spear for striking or spearing fish with. O. N. *ljóstr*, a salmon spear. Norse *ljoster, ljøster*, Dan. *lyster*, Sw. *ljuster*, vb. *Ljostra*, vb. in Norse, to spear fish. Cu. *lister, leester*. See also Worsaae, p. 260. Vb. *leister* in Sco., to strike fish with a spear or leister.

Link, *vb.* to walk briskly, smartly. Burns, 1291, 6, 5, 2. Norse *linke*, to hurry along, cp. Sw., Dan. *linke*, to limp along. Stevenson in *Ille Terrarum* 6, 3, uses *link* in the sense of "walking along leisurely," which is nearer the Dan. meaning of the word.

Lirk, *vb.* to crease, to rumple, shrivel. Ramsay, I, 307. O. N. *lerka*, to lace tight, *lirk*, sb. a crease, a fold.

Lipin, lippen, *vb.* to trust. R.R., 3501; Psalms, XVIII, 30, etc. O. N. *litna* (?), very doubtful. See B-S.

Lite, *vb.* to dye, to stain. Dalr., I, 48, 24; Douglas, IV, 190, 32. O. N. *lita*, to dye, Shetland, to *litt*. See Wall.

Litling, *sb.* dyeing. Sat. P., 48, 1. See *lit*.

Loft, *sb.* upper room, gallery. O. N. *lopt*, Norse *loft*, Aberdeen *laft*. See Skeat.

Loft, *vb.* to equip with a loft. C.S., 96. See *loft*, sb.

Lokmen, *sb. pl.* executioners. Wallace, 134. O. Dan., O. Sw. *lagman*. O. N. *lögmaðr*, literally "the law-man," was the speaker of the law. In Iceland, particularly, the *lögmaðr* was the law-speaker. In Norway a *lögman* seems also to have meant a country sheriff or officer, which comes closer to the use in Wallace. A little doubtful.

Lopprit, *pp.* clotted. Douglas, II, 157, 28; III, 306, 4. O. N. *hlaupa* (of milk), to curdle (of blood), to coagulate. So Norse *lopen, løpen* (from *læupa, løypa*), thick, coagulated. Dan. *at löbe sammen*, to curdle, *löbe*, make curdle, *löbe*, sb. curdled milk. O. N. *hlöypa mjolk*, id., literally "to make milk leap together." O. Sw. *löpa*. In Cu. milk is said to be *loppert* when curdled.

Loun, lown, *adj.* quiet, calm, sheltered. O. N. *logn*, O. Sw. *lughn*. See Wall under *lownd*.

Loup, lowp, *vb.* to leap, to jump. O. N. *hlaupa*, to leap, Norse *læupa*, run, O. Sw. *löpa*, Dan. *löbe*. Cp. Cu. *lowpy-dike*, a husband of unfaithful habits, and the secondary meanings of Norse *laupa* given in Aasen.

Loup, lowp, *sb.* a jump, a spring. Bruce, VI, 638; X, 414; Sco. Pro. 3. See the verb.

Louse, lowse, *adj.* loose, free, unfettered. Wyntoun, IX, 2, 63; Douglas, I, 95, 9; I, 95, 23. O. N. *lauss*, Norse *læus*, loose. See Wall. Sco. *to be louse*, to be abroad, about. The Norse word is similarly used. Cp. Germ. *los*, and Dan. *lös*. Waddell has the word *godlowse*, godless.

Louse, lowse, *vb.* to make loose, release. C.S., 121; Lyndsay, 460, 232; K.Q., 34. O. N. *lauss*. The O. N. vb. was *løysa*. See *louse*, adj.

Low, *vb.* to humble. R.R., 148. Same as Eng. to *lower*. So in Sco. to *hey*, to heighten.

Low, *vb.* to flame, to flare up, kindle. Dunbar, G.T., 45; Ramsay, II, 17; Psalms, LXXVI. O. N. *lǫga*, to burn with a flame, Norse *lǫga*, *laaga*, to blaze, but cp. the Sco. sb. *lowe*.

Lowe, *sb.* flame. O. N. *lǫgi*, Norse *laage*. See Skeat.

Lowne, *vb.* to shelter. Bruce, XV, 276; M. E. *lounen*, to shelter. See *lowne*, adj. Douglas, II, 236, 31, *lownit*, pp. serene, tranquil.

Luck, *vb.* to succeed. Montg., C., 643. O. N. *lukka*, reflexive, to succeed (bene succedere, Haldorson), *lukka*, sb. luck. O. Sw. *lukka*, *löcka* and *lykka*. In Scand. dial. the latter umlauted form only is found for the vb., but Norse sb. *lukka*, Dan. sb. *lykke*. Undoubtedly Norse influence in Sco.

Lucken, *vb.* to give luck, cause to succeed. Sco. formation from *luck*. Cp. *slok* and *sloken*.

Lufe, loof, *sb.* the palm of the hand. O. N *lófi*, the hollow of the hand, the palm, Norse *love*, id., Sw. dial. *love*.

Lug, *sb.* the ear. See Skeat and Wall. Cp. Norse *lugga*, to pull, and *lug* as a sb. originally "that which is pulled." In Cu. *lug* means "the handle of a pail." Compare the Eng. to *lug*, to carry.

Lythe, *vb.* to listen. Dunbar, 192, I. O. N. *hlýða*, to listen, Dan. *lytte*, O. Sw. *lyþa*, id.

Maik, *sb.* companion, partner, consort. Dunbar, T.M.W., 32; Philotus, 2. O. N. *maki*, partner, an equal, Norse *make*, Dan. *mage*, O. Sw. *maki*, M. E. *make*, consort, partner.

Maikless, *adj.* without peer. Wyntoun, IX, Prol. 48; Montg. "The Lady Margaret Montgomery," 8. O. N. *maki* + *laus*, Norse *makalæus*, Dan. *magelös*, extraordinary.

Mauch, *adj.* full of maggots. Dunbar, F., 241. O. N. *maðkr*, a maggot, W. Norse, with assimilation, *makk*, E. Norse *mark*, Dan. *madik*, Sw. dial. *mark*, O. Sw. *matk*, and *madhker*. The *k* is a diminutive ending, cp. Eng. *moth* < O. E. *maða*. In the Sco. word *ð* fell out and *a* was lengthened for compensation. Cp. Cu. *mawk*, a midge, Eng. dial. *mawkish*. Skeat cites Eng. dial. form *mad*.

Melder, *sb.* flour, meal just ground. Burns, 127, 113. O. N. *meldr*, flour, or corn in the mill, Norse *melder*, wheat about to be ground, or flour that has just been ground, *melderlas*, a load of wheat intended for the mill, *meldersekk*, a bag of flour. Cp. Cu. *melder*, the quantity of meal ground at one time.

Mense, *vb.* to do grace to. Lyndsay, 529. See *mensk*, sb. The change of *sk* to *s* is characteristic of Sco. See *mensk*.

Mensedom, *sb.* wisdom. Psalms, CV, 22. See *mensk*.

Mensk, mense, *sb.* proper conduct, more generally honor. Dunbar, T.M.W., 352; Wyntoun, VIII, 42, 143; Burns, 90, 1. O. N. *mennska*. For discussion of this word see Wall. Deriv. *menskless*, *menskful*, *menskly*.

Midding, mydding, *sb.* a midden. C.S., 12; Lyndsay, 216, 269. Dan. *mödding*, older *möghdyngh*, O. N. *mykidyngja*, Sw. dial. *mödding*, Cu. *middin*.

Mon, man, maun, *vb.* must, O. N. *monu* (*munu*), will, shall, Norse *mun*, will, but used variously. Dan. *monne, mon,* as an auxiliary vb. used very much like *do* in Eng. Sw. *mån,* Cu. *mun.* The form of the Sco. word is the same in all persons. So in Norse.

Myth, *vb.* to mark, recognize. Wallace, V, 664; Douglas, I, 28, 26. O. N. *miða,* to show, to mark a place, Norse *mida,* mark a place, *mid* sb. a mark by which to find a place. O. E. *miðan,* meant "to conceal, lie concealed," same as O. H.G. *midan,* vitare, occultare, Germ. *meiden, vermeiden,* avoid.

Neiris, *sb. pl.* the kidneys. C.S., 67. O. N. *nyra,* a kidney, Norse *nyra,* O. Dan. *nyre,* Sw. *niura,* Sw. dial. *nyra,* M. E. *nere.* Cp. Sco. *eir, an eir,* for *a neir,* as in Eng. *augur, an augur, a naugur.*

Nevin, *vb.* to name. Gol. and Gaw., 506; Howlate, II, 3, 7. O. N. *nefna,* Norse *nevna,* Dan. *nævne,* to name, O. E. *namnian.*

Nieve, neefe, neve, *sb.* the hand, the fist. O. N. *hnefi,* Norse *neve,* hand, fist, Shetland *nev,* Cu. *neif, neive, neef.* Wall considers this an unrecorded Eng. word, which is possible. Its general distribution in Scand. dial. and elsewhere in Scand. settlements, as Northern and Central England, Southern Scotland, Shetland, etc., as well as its absence in all other Gmc. languages, indicates, however, that the word is Scand. in Eng. diall.

Nout, nowt, *sb.* cattle. O. N. *naut,* cattle, Norse *næut* id. Dan. *nöd,* Sw. *noet,* Shetland *nød.* In M. Sco., also written *nolt.*

Nyk, nek, *vb.* to shake the head in denial of anything, "to nyk with nay." Gol. and Gaw, 115; Philotus, 32. Norse *nikka,* to bow slightly, *nikk,* a slight bow, Sw. *neka,* to deny, say no, M. E. *nicken.*

Nyte, *vb.* to deny. Gol. and Gaw., 889; Wyntoun, VIII, 2, 16. O. N. *næita,* to deny, refuse, Norse *neitta, neikta, nekta,* id., *neiting,* a denial, *neitan,* id., Dan. *nægte.*

Onding, *sb.* terror. Psalms, LXXXVIII, 15. See *ding.*

Onfarrand, *adj.* ill-looking. Douglas, III, 250, 26. See *farrand.*

On loft, *adv.* up. Gol. and Gaw., 485; Bruce, XIII, 652. O. N. *á loft,* up into the air. See Skeat *aloft.* Sco. Pro. 27, *upon loft,* up.

On loft, *adv.* aloud. Dunbar, T.M.W., 338. See above.

Outwale, *sb.* the best, the choice. Lyndsay, XX, 4. Eng. *out* + O. N. *val*; similar formation to Norse *udvalg, utval.*

Pirrye, *sb.* whirlwind. Sat. P., I, 178. See *bir.*

Pocknet, *sb.* from O. N. *poki,* pouch and *net,* a net. A Dumfriesshire word. Not found in any Sco. text but given by Worsaae, p. 260, and in Jamieson, where the following description is given of pocknet fishing.

> This is performed by fixing stakes or stours, as they are called, in the sand either in the channel of a river, or in the sand which is dry at low water. These stours are fixed in a line across the tideway at a distance of 46 inches from each other, about three feet high above the sand, and between every two of these stours is fixed a pocknet, tied by a rope to the top of each stour.

> P. Dorneck, Dumr. Statist. Acc., II, 1.

Quey, quoy, *sb.* a young cow, a yearling. Douglas, II, 178, 19; II, 299, 8; Burns, 595. O. N. Norse *kviga,* Dan. dial. *kvie.* Cp. Shetland *hwäi* and *kwäi.* Cu. *why, wheye* (guttural *wh*).

Quhelm, whelm, *vb.* to overturn, to turn upside down. Douglas, II, 64, 14; II, 264, 16. Burns, 66, 1, also written *quhelme, whamle, whemle.* In Cu. *whemmel,* M. E. *hwelmen.* See Skeat under *whelm.* Cp. Norse *kvelm* and *hvelm.* The O. N. *hvelfa,* N. Norse *kvelva,* means "to turn upside down."

Quyok, quyach, diminutive of *quey,* q. v.

Ra (rç), *sb.* a sail-yard. Douglas, II, 274, 16. O. N., Ic. *rá*, Dan. *raa*, Norse *raa*, Sw. *ra*, Shetland *roe*, a sail-yard.

Rad, red, *adj.* afraid. Bruce, XII, 431; Dunbar, T.M.W., 320; Montg. C. and S., 1392. O. N. *hræddr*, timid, frightened, Norse *rædd*, Dan. *ræd*, Sw. *rädd*, id., M. E. *rad.* Cp. O. N. *hræða*, to frighten, Norse *rædda*.

Radness, *sb.* timidity, fear. R.R., 1166; 1660. Deriv. from *rad*, q.v.

Radeur, *sb.* fear. L.L., 1489. Sco. formation from *rad* adj., afraid. M. E. *reddour*, *redour* is a different word from O. Fr. *reidur*, later *roideur*, see B-S.

Ragged, *adj.* full of *rag*, ragwort. Burns, 103, 85. See *ragweed*.

Ragweed, *sb.* an herb, ragwort. Burns, 6, 5, 9. O. N. *rögg*, M. E. *ragge* for which see B-S. Cp. Sw. dial. *ragg, rogga*.

Raise, raize, *vb.* to incite, stir up. Burns, 6, 5, 4; and 7, 1, 1. Used here as Sco. *bait* would be used, otherwise generally as Eng. *raise*, from O. N. *ræisa*.

Rake, raik (rçk), *vb.* to go, walk, wander, also depart. Dunbar, T.M.W., 524; Gol. and Gaw., 72; Psalms, XVIII, 10. O. N. *ræika*, to wander, Norse *ræka*, to wander about aimlessly. Cp. Cu. *rake*, a journey, "He's teann a rake ower to Kendal." See also Wall.

Ramfeezled, *adj.* exhausted, fatigued. Burns, 42, 1, 3. One of a number of words in Sco. formed with *ram*, cp. *ramshackle, ramstam, rammous*, etc. The second element probably the same as Eng. *fizzle* in the expression *to fizzle out*, fail, come to nought. See *fizz* in Skeat. See *rammys*.

Rammeist, *vb.pret.* ran wild, frenzied. Montg., F., 511. Cp. *rammous* adj. Probably the same used as a vb. Cp. Norse *ramsa*, to slash together, do a thing hurriedly, also to make a noise.

Rammys, rammous, *adj.* excited, violent. R.R., 113. O. N. *ramr, rammr*, strong, vehement, Norse *ram*, powerful, risky, hazardous. Cl. and V. cites the N. Eng. form *ram*, bitter, which is the same word.

Ramstam, *adj.* indiscreet, with an idea of rushing into anything thoughtlessly. Burns, 32, 22. O. N. *rammr*, vehement, and *stam*, stiff, hard, unbending. Cp. Cu. *ram*, strong, and *rammish*, violent, and American slang *rambunktious*, obstreperous.

Ranegill, *sb.* a scapegrace, a worthless fellow. Johnnie Gibb, 179, 11. Cp. Norse *rangel*, *ranglefant*, a loafer, rascal. Doubtful.

Rangale, *sb.* rabble, mob. Wyntoun, VIII, 36, 35; Bruce, XII, 474. O. N. *hrang*, noise, tumult, especially the noise a crowd makes.

Red, *vb.* to clear away, clear up, set to rights. R.R., 1242; Isaiah, LX, 10. O. N. *hryðja*, to clear away, Norse *rydja*, *rydda*, Sw. *rödja*, Dan. *rydde*. Cp. Eng. *rid*, O. Fr. *hredda*, O. E. *hreddan*, Norse *redda*, save, liberate. Germ. *retten* is another word.

Red up, *vb.* open up. Isaiah, XL, 3; LXII, 10. O. N. *hryðja upp*, Norse *rydde op*, clear up. In Ramsay, II, 225, *red up* pp. means dressed. See also Wall under *red*.

Redding, *sb.* growing afraid. Lyndsay, 356, 1263. See *rad*, *red*.

Reese, *vb.* to extol. Ramsay, I, 262. Eng. *raise*. See also *raise* above, as used in Burns.

Restit (very frequently reestit), *adj.* dry, withered. Burns, 6, 5. Dan. *riste*, to dry something over a *rist*, *ristet*, dried. O. N. *rist*, a gridiron. Cp. Cu. *reestit*, rancid, rusty.

Rive, ryfe, rif (rîv), *vb.* to tear, break open, cleave. Lyndsay, 434, 156; Wynyet, II, 6514; Psalms, XXIX, 5. O. N. *rifa*, to tear, Norse *riva*, *reiva*, Dan. *rive*, Sw. *rifwa*, M. E. *raven* id. Cp. Dunbar, T.M.W., 350, "rif into sondir," tear to pieces, and Norse "rive sonde." Cu. *reavv*, and *ryve*.

Rock, *sb.* a loom, spinning wheel, spinning distaff. Lyndsay, 109, 3330; Burns, 223, 112, 3; 240, 148, 1. O. N. *rokkr*, a loom, Norse *rokk*, Dan. *rok*, spinning wheel.

Rocking, *sb.* "a chat, a friendly visit at which they would spin on the rock which the visitor carried along with her" (Wagner). Burns, 4, 28. See *rock*.

Rove, rufe, *sb.* rest, repose. Montg., M.P., VI, 20; Scott, 62, 19. O. N. *ró*, Norse, Dan. *ro*, quiet, rest, Orm. *ro* (see Brate). Final epenthetic *v* also occurs in other words in Sco. Cp. *qhwov* for *qwho, cruive*, besides *crue*, etc.

Rowste, *vb.* "to cry with a rough voice." Douglas, III, 304, 11. O. N. *raust*, the voice. Dan. *röst*, Sw. *röst*, Norse *ryest*. Cp. O. N. *rausa*, to talk loud or fast. Shetland *ruz* (Cl. and V.). The Sco. vb. seems to be formed from a sb. *rowste*, which occurs in Orm.

Rowt, rout, *vb.* to cry out, roar. Lyndsay, 538, 4353; Montg., F., 501; Rolland, IV, 406. O. N. *rauta*, O. Ic. *rQuta*, to roar, to bellow, Norse *rauta, ræuta*, Sw. dial. *röta*, id. The Sw. word exhibits the E.Scand. monophthongation, which took place in Dan. about 900.

Rowt, *sb.* loud clamor. Poet. R., 157; Ramsay, I, 251. See vb. *rowt*.

Ruckle, rickle, *sb.* a little heap of anything. Lyndsay, 539, 4356; Burns, 596; M.W., 114, 3. See Wall under *rook*. *Ruckle* is the form of the word in Edinburgh dial. May be Eng. Skeat considers Eng. *ruck* Scand. and *rick* Eng., but in Scotland the one may be simply a variant of the other, not necessarily a doublet. Cp. *fill* and *full*.

Ruik, a heap. Lyndsay, 454, 2079; 494, 3075. Spelled *ruck*, meaning "a cock of hay," in Ramsay's "The Gentle Shepherd," 160. See Wall, under *rook*. Cp. Cu. *ruck*, the chief part, the majority.

Roop and Stoop. Ramsay, II, 527; M.W. 203, 8; 214, 5. Cp. *rubb og stubb*, every particle. Aasen defines "löst og fast, smaat og stort, selja rubb og stubb," sell everything, dispose of all one has; literally "stump and piece," "rump and stump." Used exactly the same way in Sco. Of very frequent occurrence in this sense in Norway.

Rund, roond, roon, *sb.* the border of a web, the edge. Burns, 596. O. N. *rond*, rim, border, Dan. *rand*, a line, seam, the border, Norse *rand*, *rond*, a streak, seam, edge, border. Cp. Cu. *randit*, streaked, Norse *randet*, id.

Runsik, *vb.* to ransack. Wallace, VII, 120. O. N. *rannsaka*, to search a house, Norse *ransaka*, from *ran*, house, and *saka, söka*, seek. See Skeat, and Kluge and Lutz.

Rusare, *sb*, a flatterer. R.R., 3356. See *ruse*.

Ruse, roose, russ (rŭs), *vb.* to praise, to boast, pride oneself. Douglas, II, 57, 8; Rolland, I, 389; R.R., 2823. O. N. *rósa*, older *hrósa*, to praise, Norse *rosa*, Dan. *rose*, Sw. *rosa*, M. E. (*h*)*rosen*, Lincolnshire *rose*, *reouse*, Cu. *roose*.

Ruse, *sb.* praise, a boast. Dunbar, T.M.W., 431; Sat. P., 12, 17. O. N. *hrós*, praise, Norse, Dan. *ros*.

Saikless, *adj.* innocent. Lyndsay, 545, 4563. O. N. *saklauss*, O. E. *saclças*. The O. E. word is a loan-word from O. Nh. See Steenstrup, 210-211. In modern Eng. dial. the form is generally *sackless*.

Saiklessness, *sb.* innocence, innocency. Psalms, XXVI, 6, 11; LXXIII, 13. See *saikless*.

Sait, *sb.* session, court. Dunbar, 79, 41. O. N. *sæti*, seat, sitting, Norse *sæte*, id. See Skeat under *seat*.

Saucht, *adj.* reconciled, also at ease, undisturbed, tranquil. Bruce, N, 300; Douglas, II, 91, 22. O. E. *saht*, borrowed from O. N. See Kluge, P. G.² I, 934. For discussion of O. E. *seht* and *sehtian* see Steenstrup, 181-182. In Howlate, III, 16, *sacht* vb. pret., made peace.

Say, *sb.* a milk-pail, also tub. Jamieson, Dumfries. O. N. *sár*, a large cask, Norse *saa*, a pail, a water-bucket, a wooden tub, Dan. *saa*, *vandsaa*, waterpail, Sw. *så*, id.

Scait, *sb.* the skate fish. Dunbar, 261, 9. O. N. *skata*, Norse *skata*, the skate, M. E. *scate*. Ir. *scat*, *sgat*, id., is a loan-word from O. N. (Cp. Craigie, p. 163). O. N. *sk* becomes quite regularly *sg* in Ir. and Gael. Cp. also *sgeir* < *skar*. Cu. *skeatt* exhibits regular i-fracture from older *a*.

Scaith, scath, *vb.* to injure. Bruce, IV, 363; XII, 392; R. R., 1323. Not from O. Nhb. *sceðða*, but from O. N. *skaða*, Norse *skade*, with which the vowel corresponds.

Scar, *sb.* a precipitous bank of earth, a bare place on the side of a steep hill, a cliff. Ramsay, II, 205; Burns, 10, 11. Also written *skard*, *scair*, *scaur*. O. N. *sker*, a skerry, an isolated rock in the sea. Norse *skjær*, a projecting cliff, a bank of rocky ground, Dan. *skjær*, *skær*, a rock in the water near the land, Sw. *skär*, M. E. *sker*, *scerre*. Cp. Cu. *skerr*, a precipice. The fundamental idea is "something cut apart, standing by itself." Root the same as in the Norse *skera*, to cut, Eng. *shear* and *shore*, sea-*shore*. Cp. the O. E. vb. *scorian* cited by Sweet.

Scarth, *sb.* the cormorant. Dunbar, T.M.W., 92; F., 194; Douglas, I, 46, 15. O. N. *skarfr*, Norse *skarv*, cormorant. Shetland, *scarf*.

Schoir, *sb.* a threat, menace. Bruce, VI, 621; Gol. and Gaw., 103. B-S. derive from O. Sw. *skorra*, O. N. *skera*.

Scol, *vb.* to wish one health, an expression used in drinking, just as the Norse *skaal* is used. Montg. S., 69, 13. O. N. *skal*, Norse *skaal*, a drinking cup. Cp. Sco. *skull*, a goblet. Ir.-Gael. *scala*, *sgaile*, a beaker, is a Norse loan-word (Craigie).

Scoug, scog, *vb.* to shelter. M.W., 20, 19; Isaiah, XVIII, 6. O. N. *skuggi*, shade, Norse *skugge*, to shade, Sw. *skugga*, sb., Dan. *skygge*, to shade. Spelled *scug* also in Sco.

Scratch, *sb.* an hermaphrodite. Jamieson. O. N. *skratti*, a monster. This form exists in Yorkshire, otherwise the form in Eng. dial. is *scrat*. See Wall.

Scrip, a coarse or obscene gesture. Wallace, VI, 143. Probably from O. N. *skripi*. Cp. *skripatal*, scurrilous language, *skripalæti*, buffoonery, scurrilous gestures. With the Sco. word cp. the Norse *skripa*, vb., *skripa*, sb. f., and Ic. *skrípr*, sb. m. See Aasen.

Scud, *vb.* to hurry away, hasten on. Burns, 55, 1, 4. Eng. *scud* Skeat derives from Dan. *skyde*, Sw. *skutta*. The Sw. form is nearest, the Dan. form shows umlaut. The corresponding O. E. word is *scçotan*.

Scudler, a male kitchen servant. Wallace, 5, 10, 27. Cp. O. N. *skutilsvæinn*, a page at a royal table. *Skutil* is the same as O. E. *scutel*, a dish, a trencher. In O. N. it means also "a small table." The unpalatalized *sc*, as well as the usage, would indicate that the word is a loan-word.

Seir, ser, *adj.* various, separate. Rolland, Prol., 295; R.R., 990; "Freires of Berwick," 321. O. N. *sér*, for oneself, separately. Originally the dative of the refl. pron., but used very frequently as an adverb.

Semeley, *adv.* proper, looking properly. Wallace, I, 191; Wyntoun, IX, 26, 53. *Seimly, semely-farrand*, good-looking, handsome, also means "in proper condition." Redundant, since *semely* and *farrand* in Sco. mean the same. O. N. *sæmiligr.* See Skeat.

Shacklet, *adj.* crooked, distorted. Burns, 322, I, 7. O. N. *skakkr*, skew, wry, distorted, *skakki-fótr*, wry leg, Norse *skakk*, crooked, so Sw. dial. *skak*, Dan. *skak*, slanting. The palatal *sh* is unusual, but cp. *dash* from *daska*. Norse words generally preserve *sk* in all positions, genuine Eng. words do not. See Part I, 12 and 13.

Shiel, *sb.* shelter, protection. Burns, 226, 119, 3. O. N, *skjól*, shelter, cover, refuge, Norse *skjul, skjol*, pron. *shul, shol*, Dan. *skjul*, id., *skjule*, to conceal. *Shielin*, sb. shelter, may be formed from the vb.

Shore, *vb.* to threaten. Ramsay, I, 261. Origin rather doubtful. Has been considered Scand. See *schoir.*

Sit (sît), *vb.* to grieve. Wallace, I, 438. O. N. *sýta*, Norse *syta*, to care. See *syte*, sb.

Sitefull, *adj.* sorrowful, distressing. Douglas, I, 40, 19. Cp. Norse *suteful.* See *syte*, sb.

Skail, skale, scale, *vb.* to scatter, disperse, dismiss, part, leave. A very common word. O. N. *skilja*, separate, O. Dan. *skiliæ*, Norse, *skilja*, Dan. *skille*, Sw. dial. *skila*. The long vowel is unusual. Cp. *skeely* in N. Sco. from O. N. *skilinn*. The same change of *i* to an e-vowel is observed in *gleit* and *quey.*

Skail, *sb.* a storm, a strong wind that "skails." Isaiah, XXVIII, 2. See *skail*, vb.

Skath, skaith, scaith, *sb.* harm, misery. O. N. *skaði*, harm, damage, Norse *skade*, id., Dan. *skade*, O. E. *sceaða.*

Skant, *sb.* want, poverty. Burns, 290, I, 3. O. N. *skammt.* See Skeat. Cp. *skerum skamti*, in short measure.

Skantlin, *sb.* little. Burns, 5, 5, 7. As adv. generally *skantlins, scantlings*, scarcely. O. N. *skamt.*

Skantly, *adv.* with difficulty, hardly. C.S., 69. See *skant.*

Skar, *sb.* a scarecrow, a fright. Lyndsay, 437, 1633. From vb. *skar*, to frighten, Eng. *scare*, M. E. *skerren*. O. N. *skirra*. See Skeat.

Skeigh, *adj.* originally meant timid, then very frequently, dainty, nice, finally, proud. Dunbar, T.M.W., 357. Burns, 193, 46, I. Norse *sky*, Dan. *sky*, adj. and also vb. *sky*, to avoid. B-S. compares Sw. *skygg* also, which is the same word, but the vowel is long. The Sco. word, furthermore, seems to suggest an older diphthong. It could, however, not be O. E. *sceah*, which gave M. E. *scheah* and should have become *schee* in N. Sco. Doubtful.

Sker, *adj.* timid, easily frightened. Dunbar, T.M.W., 357; Lyndsay, 227, 126. O. N. *skjarr*, shy, timid, Sw. dial. *skar*, M. E. *scer*, Cu. *scar*, wild.

Skewyt, *vb. pret.* turned obliquely. Wallace, IX, 148. O. N. *skæifr*, O. Ic. *skeifr*, oblique, Norse *skæiv*, *skjaiv*, crooked, Dan. *skjæv*. The Dan word exhibits monophthongation of *æi* to *æ* (not to *e*, *i*, as in *sten*).

Skill, *sb.* motive, reason. Gol. and Gaw., 147; Bruce, I, 214, 7. See Skeat, and Kluge and Lutz. In Dunbar, 307, 63, "did nane skill," did not do a wise thing.

Skog, scoug, *sb.* place of retreat, shelter, protection. Dalr., I, 30, 29; Isaiah, XXXII, 2. O. N. *skuggi*, shade, Norse *skugge*, O. Sw. *skuggi*.

Skogy, *adj.* shady. Douglas, III, 1, 21, 16. See *scoug*.

Skrech, skrik, *sb.* a scream, yell. C.S., 39; Rolland, IV, 336. O. N. Norse *skrik*, a cry, a yell, *skrikja*, vb. Dan. *skrig*. Cu. *skrike* to scream. Eng. *shriek* < O. E. **scrician*.

Skryp, *sb.* bag. Dunbar, F., 509. O. N. *skreppa*, a bag, Norse *skreppa*, Dan. *skreppe*, Sw. *skräppa*, id.

Skugg, *sb.* a shadow. Dunbar, III, 24, 12. O. N. *skuggi*. See *skog*. Cp. *skog*, vb. to hide. Isaiah, XXVIII, 15.

Skyle, *vb.* to hide, cover. Jamieson, quotation from Henryson. O. N. *skjúla*, O. Ic. *skjóla*, to screen, shelter, Norse *skjula*, Dan. *skjul*, Sw. *skyla*, Fer. *skỹla*, Shetland *skail*, *skol*, cover, protect. Our word corresponds most closely to the Fer. word. Both are developed out of O. N. *skjúla*. Cp. O. N. *mjúkr* > *meek*, in standard Eng. Norse *skjula* has preserved the original unumlauted vowel. The O. N. word was pronounced *sk-iula* or *sk-júla*. Cp. *skjenka*, which is N. Norse dial. *sheinka*. From *skj* developed *sh* in *shielin*.

Skyrin, *adj.* shining, conspicuous because of brightness, showy. Burns, 210, 87, 3. O. N. *skirr*, clear, bright, *skira*, to make clear, *skýra*, to purify. (Cp. Norse *skjerr-torsdag*, O. N. *skiriþorsdagr*, Maundy Thursday.) O. E. *scir* > N. Eng. *sheer*.

Slaik, *vb.* to smooth, to lick. L.L., 457, 2173. O. N. *slæikja*, to lick, Norse *sleikja*, Dan. *slikke*, O. Sw. *slekia*, Sw. dial. *släkja*. The Eng. word *slick*, with a short vowel, corresponds exactly to the Dan. word, but may be native. Cp. M. L. G. *slicken*. *Slikke* in Dan. may be a loan-word from L. G. The Sco. *slaik* corresponds in every way to the O. N., and is certainly a loan-word proved by quality and quantity of vowel.

Slak, *sb.* a pit, a hollow in the ground, hollow place. Bruce, XIV, 536; R.R., 769. O. N. *slakki*, a slope, Norse *slakke*, Dan. *slank*. Exhibits W. Scand. assimilation of *nk* to *kk*. Cu. *slack*, a shallow dell (Dickinson), Kent, *slank*.

Sle, *adj.* experienced, skillful. Bruce, XVI, 355; XVII, 44. O. N. *slægr*, O. Ic. *slægr*, Eng. *sly*. See Skeat.

Sleek, *adj.* neat, prancing, said of a horse. Burns, 7, 1, 1. O. N. *slikr*, smooth. *Sleikit*, smooth, Dunbar, 567, 38; Burns, 117, 114. See Skeat, under *sleek*, *slick*.

Sleuth, *sb.* track. Bruce, VII, 1 and 44. O. N. *slóð*, track, trail. Cp. Norse *slod*, *slode*.

Sloke, *vb.* to quench. Isaiah, I, 2, 3; and 49, 26. O. N. *slökva*, to quench. O. Ic. *slækva*, Norse *slökka*, id. The word does not show the Scand. umlaut *o* > *ö*. Cu. *sleck* has further developed the umlaut *ö* to *e*. Cp. O. Ic. *æ* < O. Nh. *æ*. All such words in Norse exhibit the intermediate stage *ö* up to the present time. In Ic. the *ö* developed to *æ*, in the first half of the 13th century. (See Noreen P. G.² I, 529.) In later O. Nhb. also *æ* > *e*.

Sloken, slokyn, *vb.* to quench, to satisfy. Dunbar, T.M.W., 283; K.Q., 42; M.W., 116, 35. O. N. *slokna*, Norse *slokna*, inchoative of *slökva*. It may, however, be an infinitive in *en* from *slökkva*, see *slock*.

Slokning, *sb.* the act of quenching, also the power of quenching. Douglas, II, 26, heading of Chapter XII; Montg. C. and S., 1377. Pr. p., see *sloken*. Cp. O. N. *slokning*, Dan. *slukning*.

Slonk, *sb.* a ditch, a depression in the land, also a slope on the mountain side. Winyet, II, 19, 5; Wallace, III, 4. Dan. *slank*, a depression in the land, a hollow, O. N. *slakki*, Norse *slakke*. The non-assimilation proves E.Scand. source. Cp. Sw. dial. *slakk* adj. bending, e.g., "bakken jär no na slakk," the hill slopes a great deal, again a W. Scand. form in Sw. dial. The word is probably related to Eng. *slack*, loose, lax, Dan. *slak*, Norse *slâk*.

Slut, *sb.* a slattern, an untidy woman. Dunbar, 119, 71. O. N., O. Ic. *slöttr*. See Skeat.

Smaik, *sb.* a coward. Sat. P., 39, 175; Lyndsay, 425, 1320, and 434, 1562. O. N. *smöykr*, adj. timid, M. L. G. *smeker* means "a flatterer," besides the vowel, as well as the final *r* of the L. G. word, is against a L. G. origin of the Sco. word. The Sco. *ai* indicates an original diphthong. Cp. Cu. *smaik* applied to a small boy, or any small being.

Snape-dike, *sb.* an enclosure. Jamieson, Ayr. Cp. O. N. *snap*, a pasture for cattle, especially a winter pasture (Haldorson), *snapa*, vb. to nibble, M. E. *snaipen*. The vowel in the Sco. word proves an original open *a*, hence it is from the vb. *snapa*. O. N. *snap*, sb. would have given *snăp*. Our word is *snǫp*.

Snib, sneb, *vb.* to snub, check, reprove. Sat., P., 33, 18; L.L., 3387. Dan. *snibbe*, M. E. *snibben*. Eng. *snub* and M. E. *snubben* correspond to O. N. *snubba* with original unumlauted vowel.

Snite, *vb.* to blow the nose, to snuff a candle. Jamieson. O. N. *snýta*, Norse *snyta*, used exactly the same way, Dan. *snyde*. Sw. *snute* and M. L. G. *snuten* have unumlauted vowel which would have given *snoot*, *snowt*, or *snoit* in Sco.

Sock, *vb.* to examine, investigate. Fergusson, 169. Probably from O. N. *sækja*, to seek, Norse *söka*, *sökja*, Dan. *söge* since O. Nhb. *sæca* later became *sçca* and developed as W. S. *sécan*.

Solande, *sb.* a soland goose. Dalr., I, 25, 1. O. N. *súla* + *n* (Skeat). The *d* is epenthetic. The *n* is the post-positive definite article, a peculiarly Scand. characteristic.

Sop, *sb.* a round, compact body. Bruce, III, 47. O. N. *soppr*, a ball (Skeat), Norse *sopp*, id. Cp. Cu. *sop*, "a milk-maid's cushion for the head."

Soum, *sb.* The rope or chain a plow is drawn by. Dunbar, III, 126, 21. O. N. *saumr*, a seam, trace. In Bruce, X, 180, *hede-soyme*, sb. the trace.

Soym, *sb.* trace of a cart. Bruce, X, 233. From O. N. *saumr*, a seam (Skeat), Norse *saum*, Dan. *söm*. For *oy* in place of *ou*, as we should expect, cp. *gowk* and *goilk*, *lowp* and *loip*, etc., and the Norse *laupa* and *loipa*.

Spae, spa, *vb.* to prophesy. Douglas, II, 142, 2; II, 2; Burns, 37, 2, 2. O. N. *spá*, to prophesy, Norse *spaa*, Dan. *spaa*, id. Cp. *spaamand*, *spaafolk*, and Sco. *spaeman*, *spaefolk*, *spaewife*.

Spay, spe, *sb.* prophecy, omen, augury. Dalr., II, 5, 8; Isaiah, XLVII, 12. O. N. *spá*, a prophecy. *Vǫluspá*, the vala's prophecy, M. E. *spa*.

Spaequean, *sb.* fortune teller, spaewife. Isaiah, XLVII. O. N. *spákona*, a woman who spaes. The compound may, however, be Sco.

Spale, *sb.* lath, chip, splinter. R.R., 1979; Burns, 132, 114. Norse *spela*, *spila*, *speil*, a splinter, a chip, also *spol*. O. N. *spölr*, a rail, bar, lattice work, sometimes means "a short piece of anything." Cu. *speal*. The O. E. word is *speld*. Cp. Fr. *espalier*.

Spenn, *vb.* to button, to lace. Jamieson. O. N. *spenna*, to clasp. Norse *spenna*, lace, *spenne* sb. a buckle, Dan. *spænde*, Sw. *spänne*, to lace. The O. E. word is *spannan*, without umlaut. The meaning as well as the form of the Sco. word is Scand.

Sprack, *adj.* lively, animated. Jamieson. O. N. *sprǽkr*, quick, strong, sprightly, Norse *spræk*, spry, nimble, Dan. *spræk*, M. E. *sprac*. This is one of a few undoubted Scand. words found in South Eng. diall.

Spil, *sb.* a stake. Douglas, III, 250, 16. O. N. **spílr*, variant of *spölr*. Cp. Norse *spil*, in the diall. of Western Norway. See *spale*.

Sprattle, *vb.* to walk through mud, to scramble through wet and muddy places as the result of which one's clothes become soiled. Burns, 10, 11, 3; also 68, 1, 3. O. N. *spretta*, Norse *spretta* to spurt, sputter, splash, Sw. *spritte*. On assimilation of *nt*, cp. *sprent*. The *l* is frequentative. Exhibits characteristic Sco. change of *e* to *a* before t. Cp. *wat* for *wet*, *swat* for *sweat*.

Sprent, *vb.* to start, spring. Wallace, N, 23. O. Dan. *sprenta*, spurt out, spring, start, O. N. *spretta*, Norse *spretta*, shoot forth, spurt. In Cu. a pen is said to *sprent* when it scatters the ink over the paper. So in Norse. The Sco. word agrees more closely in meaning with the Norse than with the Dan. but exhibits E. Scand. non-assimilation of *nt* to *tt* which took place in Norse before 1000. Sw. diall. which otherwise have many W. Scand. characteristics have both *sprenta* and *spritta*. The word *sprætte* also occurs in later Dan.

Sprent, *sb.* a spring, as the back spring of a knife. Wallace, IV, 238. See *sprent*, vb.

Stakker, stacker, *vb.* to stagger. Brace, II, 42; Gol. and Gaw., II, 25. O. N. *stakra*. See B-S. under M. E. *stakerin*. Cp. Norse *stakra*, to stagger, to fall.

Stang, *vb.* to sting. R.R., 771. O. N. *stanga*, to prick, goad, also to butt, Norse *stanga*, Dan. *stange*, id., M. E. *stangen*.

Stapp, *vb.* to put into, to stuff, fill. Dunbar, T.M.W., 99; Montg. C. and S., 1552; Isaiah, VI, 6; M.W. 21, 12. O. N. *stappa*, to stamp down, Norse *stappa*, to stuff, fill, same as O. E. *stempan*, Eng. *stamp*, Dan. *stampe*. The assimilated form *stampa* occurs in Norse beside *stappa*. The usage in Sco. is distinctively Norse and the vowel is the Norse vowel. Not the same as Eng. *stop*, O. E. *(for)stoppian* in Leechdoms. With the last cp. Dan. *stoppe* used just like Eng. *stop*.

Starn, *sb.* the helm of a vessel. Dunbar, F., 450. O. N. *stjorn*, steerage, helm, Norse *stjorn*, vb. *stjorna*, to steer, cognate with Eng. *steer*, O. E.

styrian. For a similar difference between the Eng. and the Norse word cp. Eng. *star* and Norse *stjerne.*

Starr, *sb.* sedge, heavy coarse grass. Jamieson. See Wall under *star.*

Stern, starn, *sb.* star. C.S., 48; Dunbar, G.T. 1; Lindsay, 239, 492. O. N. *stjarna,* Dan. *stjerne,* star, Norse *stjerna.*

Stert, *vb.* to start, rush. Poet. R., 109, 8. O. N. *sterta.* For discussion of this word see Skeat.

Stoop, *sb.* See *roop.*

Storkyn, *vb.* to become rigid, stiffen. Dunbar, 248, 48. Norse *storkna,* coagulate, become rigid. See Wall under *storken.*

Stot, *sb.* a young bull, bullock. Montg., C. and S., 1099; A.P.B. 1, 306; Burns, 231, 129, 4. Stratmann derives M. E. *stot,* "buculus," from Sw. *stut*; and *stot,* "caballus," from O. E. *stotte.* O. N. *stútr* is rather the source of the former. Norse *stut,* Dan. *stud.*

Stour, *sb.* a pole. Douglas, III, 248, 27. O. N. *staur,* a pole, a stake, Norse *staur,* Sw. *stör,* Dan. and Dano-Norse *stör.* See the quotation under *pocknet.*

Stowit, *pt. p.* cutoff, cropped. Douglas, III, 42, 3. O. N. *stúfa,* a stump, *stýfa,* to cut off, Dan. *stuve,* Sw. *stuf,* a piece left after the rest has been cut away, *styva,* to crop, O. Sw., Sw. dial. *styva, stuva,* id. An O. E. *styfician,* to root up, occurs once (Leechdoms). See B-T.

Stowp, *sb.* a pitcher, a beaker. Dunbar, 161, 26. O. N. *staup,* a beaker, a cup, Norse *staup,* id., Dan. *stöb,* O. E. *stçap,* O. H.G. *stouf.*

Stray, strae, stra, *sb.* straw. O. N. *strá,* Dan., Norse *straa,* Sw. *strå,* Cu. *strea.*

Stroup, (strŭp), *sb.* the spout of a kettle or pump. Burns, 602; Jamieson. O. N. *strjúpi,* the spurting trunk, Norse *strupe* and *striupe,* the throat, gullet, Dan. *strube,* id., M. E. *strŭpe,* the throat.

Studie, *sb.* anvil. Dunbar, 141, 52. The word rhymes with *smidy.* See *styddy.*

Styddy, studdie, stuthy, *sb.* anvil. Douglas, III, 926, 9; III, 180, 26; Dunbar 141, 52. See also Burns, 502. O. N. *steði,* a stithy, an anvil. Norse *sted.* Sw. *städ.* Exhibits change of ð to *d* which is a Sco. characteristic, but does not often take place in Norse words. See, too, Cu. *stiddy,* *steady.*

Sumph, *sb.* a blunt fellow. Burns, 98, 1. Norse *sump,* a bungler, a simpleton, *sumpa,* vb. to entangle, put into disorder, *sump,* a disordered mass. Cu. *sumph.* M. L. G. *sump,* and Dan. *sump* do not seem to be quite the same.

Swarf, *vb.* originally to turn, then to overturn, fall over, fall. Burns, 211, 87, 4. O. N. *svarfa,* to turn aside, to be turned upside down, Sw. *swarfve,* Norse *svarva,* turn, swing about, Dan. *svarve* or *svarre.* Eng. *swerve* does not quite correspond. O. E. *sweorfan* meant "to file, polish," O. S. *swerban,* to wipe off, polish, O. F. *swerva,* to creep.

Swage, swey, *vb.* sway, waver, also turn, make turn. Sat. P., 5, 8; Douglas, II, 104, 12. O. N. *svæigja,* to bend, to sway, Dan. *sveie,* Sw. dial. *sväiga,* Norse *sveigja.*

Syte, *sb.* grief, suffering. Lyndsay, 273, 333. Montg., M.P., V, 14. O. N. *sýta,* to wail, *sýting,* sb., *sút,* grief, affliction, Norse *sut,* care, *syta,* to care. Skeat cites *sut* (in list) which would exactly correspond to the O. N. sb. Brate accepts an O. N. sb. *syt.*

Tait, *adj.* foul. Montg., F., 755. O. N. *tað.* The change of *ð* to *t* is unusual. See Wall.

Tangle, *sb.* seaweed, stalk of a seaweed. Dalr., I, 62, 1; Burns, 91, 2, 2. O. N. *þöngul,* tangle, seaweed. Cp. *þönglabakki,* Tangle-hill, name of a place in Iceland. In Norse *tangel* same as Eng. *tangle, entangle.*

Tangling, *pr. p.,* *adj.* clinging, intertwining. Burns, 60, 3, tangling roots, clinging together in tangles. See *tangle.*

Tarn, *sb.* a small lake. Jamieson. O. N. *tjörn,* a small lake, Norse *tjönn, tjörn,* Sw. *tjärn,* M. E. *terne,* a lake. Particularly Sco. and N.W. Eng. Cp. Shetland *shon, shoden,* a pool, a little lake. The last example exhibits W. Norse change of *rn* to *dn.* The form *tjödn* occurs in Sogn, Norway.

Tath, *sb.* Jamieson. O. N. *tað.* See Wall.

Teal, till, *vb.* to entice. Wallace, VI, 151, and Jamieson. O. N. *tæla*, to entice, related to Norse *telja*. Sco. *tealer*, *sb.* Jamieson. The form in *i* is strange.

Teynd, teind, *sb.* tithe. C.S., 123; Lyndsay, 152, 4690; Rolland, I, 546. O. N. *tíund*, the tenth, the tithe, Norse *tiende*, Dan. *tiende*, the regular ordinal of *ti*.

Tha, *dem. pron.* these, those. Same form in all cases. Wallace, X, 41; Wyntoun, I, 1, 6. O. N. *þeir*.

Theck, *vb.* to thatch. Ramsay, II, 224. Has been taken as a loan-word from O. N. *þekja*, to thatch, Norse *tekka*, Sw. *täcka*. Cp. O. E. *þeccan*. *Theck* probably comes from O. Nhb. *þecca*.

Thir, *dem. pron.* these, those. Bruce, I, 76; Dunbar, G.T., 127; Lyndsay, 4, 20, 1175; R.R., 108. O. N. *þeir*. Cp. M. E. *þir*, *þer*, those, Cu. *thur*.

Thra, *adj.* eager. Bruce, XVIII, 71. O. N. *þrár*, obstinate, persistent, Norse *traa*, untiring, also wilful, Sw. dial. *trå*, M. E. *þra*, bold, strong, *thraly*, adv. Wyntoun, II, 8, 55; VII, 8, 186. See Wall. Skeat cites Eng. dial. *thro*.

Thra, *adv.* boldly. Dunbar, T.M.W., 195. See above, *thra*.

Thraif, *sb.* two stooks or twenty-four sheaves of grain. Dunbar, 228. O. N. *þrefi*, a number of sheaves, Dan. *trave*, Sw. *trafwe*, twenty sheaves of grain, M. E. *þrâve*, a bundle, a number, Cu. *threve*, *threeav*.

Threave, *sb.* a crowd, a large number. Ramsay, II, 463. The same word as *thraif*, q.v.

Thrist, *vb.* to thrust, push, also means to clasp. Bruce, XIII, 156; R.R. 12, 9; Rolland, IV, 590. O. N. *þrýsta*, to thrust, force, Norse *trysta*, to press together, M. E. *þrîsten*, *þrȳstan*. Lyndsay also uses the word in the sense of "to pierce."

Thwaite, *sb.* originally a small piece of cleared land on which a house was built, a cottage with its paddock. O. N. *þvæit*, O. Ic. *þveit*. Northwest England *thwaite*, Norse *tveit*, *tvæit*, Dan. *tved*. Occurs in a number of place-names in S. Scotland, especially in Dumfriesshire. Its form is

Norse not Dan. *Thweet* or *thwet* would correspond to the Dan. word, but see also Part III, 1.

Tit, tyt, adv. soon, quickly. Bruce, II, 4; IV, 289. O. N. *títt*, adv. frequently, in quick succession, "höggva hart ok títt." The Sco. word comes from this O. N. form, which is simply the neuter inflected form of *tiðr*, adj. meaning "customary, familiar." The comparative *titter* often means "rather" in Sco., like Eng. *sooner*. Cp. Cu. "I'd as tite deat as nut," "I'd as lief do it as not."

Tithand, titand, *sb.* news, tidings. Bruce, IV, 468; Lyndsay, 341, 720. O. N. *tiðindi*, news, Norse *tidende*, id., Dan. *tidende*, Orm. *tiþennde*. Of O. E. *tidung* > *tidings* Bosworth says: "the use of the word, even if its form be not borrowed from Scand., seems to have Scand. influence."

Titlene, *sb.* the hedge sparrow. C.S., 38. O. N. *titlingr*, a tit, a sparrow.

Toym, tume, *sb.* leisure. Bruce, V, 64, 2, XVII, 735. O. N. *tóm*, leisure (Skeat).

Traist, *vb.* to trust. Bruce, I, 125; XVII, 273; Rolland, I, 27. *Trast*, *adj.* secure, *traist*, *sb.* confidence. Lindsay, 229, 195. *Traisting*, *sb.* confidence, reliance, L.L., 25. Cp. O. N. *tröysta*, *adj. traustr*, and Eng. *trust*, M. E. *trusten*. I do not at present understand the relation between the forms in *e*, and these in *u* and *ou*.

Trig, *adj.* trim, neat, handsome. M.W., 159, 26. O. N. *tryggr*, true, trusty, unconcerned, *trygging*, security, O. Dan. *trygd*, *trugd*, confidence (Schlyter), Norse *trygg*, secure, unconcerned, confident, *tryggja*, to consider secure, *tryggja sek*, feel secure, Dan. *tryg*, fearless, confident. Cp. Cu. *trig*, tight, well-fitted, "trig as an apple." The M. E. *trig* means faithful, see B-S. Ramsay, II, 526, uses the adv. *trigly* in the sense of "proudly."

Twist, *sb.* twig, branch. Bruce, VII, 188; Montg., C. and S., Irving, 468. O. N. *kvistr*, a twig, O. Dan., *quist*, Norse, Dan. *kvist*, Sw. *quist*, id. For the change of *kv* (*kw*) to *tw* cp. Norse, Dan. *kviddre*, Sw. *quittra*, Du. *kwittern* with Eng. *twitter*, and *kj* to *tj* in W. Norse. A regular change.

Tyne, *vb.* lose, impair, destroy. C.S., 3; Wyntoun, IX, 21, 14; R.R. 779. O. N. *týna*, to lose, destroy, Norse *tyna*, to lose, sometimes impair, Sw. dial. *tyna*, to destroy.

Tynsell, tynsale, *sb.* loss. Bruce, V, 450, XIX, 449; R.R., 505. In Wyntoun, IX, 3, 25, it means "delay, loss of time," frequently means "loss of life, slaughter." M. E. *tinsel*, loss, ruin, probably a Sco. formation from *tyne*, to lose, similarly in Norse *tynsell*, loss (not frequent), from *tyna*.

Tynsale, *vb.* to lose, suffer loss. Bruce, XIX, 693. See the sb.

Tytt, *adj.* firm, tight. Wallace, VII, 21, 2. O. N. *þittr*, tight, close, Norse, *tett* or *titt*, Dan. *tæt*, Sw. *tät*, close together, tight, Eng. dial. *theet*. The long vowel in *theet* is unusual.

Ug, *vb.* to dislike, abhor. Winyet, II, 31, 32; Scott, 71, 119. O. N. *ugga*, abhor, Norse *ugga*, see B-S.

Ugsum, *adj.* fearful. Sat. P., 3, 135. See *ug*. *Ougsum*, Howlate, I, 8, means "ugly."

Underlie, *adj.* wonderful. Gau, 29, 24. Dan. *underlig*, Norse, *underleg*, O. N. *underlegr*, wonderful, shows Scand. loss of *w* before *u*. The O. E. word is *wundorlic*, cp. Scand. *ulf*, Eng. *wolf*. The word is Dan. in Gau.

Unfleckit, *adj.* unstained. Psalms, XXIV, 4. See *fleckerit*.

Unganand (gçn.), *adj.* unfit, unprepared. Douglas, II, 48, 16. See *ganand*.

Unrufe, *sb.* restlessness, vexation. Gol. and Gaw., 499. See *rove*, sb. Cp. Norse *uro*, restlessness, noise, Dan. *uro*, id.

Unsaucht, *adj.* disturbed, troubled. Gol. and Gaw., II, 12. See *saucht*.

Upbigare, *sb.* a builder. Winyet, II, 3, 4. See *big*. Cp. Norse *bygga up*.

Uploip, *vb.* leap up. Montg., M.P., III, 33. See *loup*. On this change of *ou* to *oi* cp. the same word in Norse, *laupa* and *loipa*.

Vath, waith, *sb.* danger. Bruce, V, 418; Wallace, IX, 1737. O. N. *váði*, harm, mishap, disaster, Dan. *vaade*, danger, adversity, Sw. *våde*, an unlucky accident, M. E. *wâþe*, peril. Does not seem to exist in the modern diall.

Vitterly, *adv.* certainly. Bruce, IV, 771; X, 350. O. N. *vitrliga*, wisely, Dan. *vitterlig*, well-known, undoubted, M. E. *witerliche*, certainly.

Vyndland, *pr. p.* whirling around. Bruce, XVII, 721. O. N. *vindla*, to wind up. Norse *vindel*, a curl, anything twisted or wound. Cu. *winnel*. Cp. Dan. *vindelbugt*, a spiral twist. Skeat cites provincial Eng. *windle*, a wheel for winding yarn.

Wag, *vb.* to totter, walk unsteady. Dunbar, 120, 98. Norse, *vagga*, to swing, rock, sway, O. N. *vaga*, to waddle. See further Skeat.

Waggle, *vb.* to wag, sway from side to side, wabble. M.W., 16, 23; 51, 5. Sw. dial. *vagla*, *vackla*, to reel, Norse *vakla*, id. May be taken as a Sco. frequentative of *wag*, q.v. Not to be derived from the L. G. word. Confined to the Scand. settlements.

Wailie, *adj.* excellent. Burns, 179, 2, 3, and 8, 7. See *wale*, sb.

Wailit, *adj.* choice, fashionable, excellent. Rolland, I, 64. See *wail*, vb.

Wale, *vb.* to select, choose. Douglas, III, 3, 21; Dunbar, G.T., 186. Probably from the noun *wale*, choice. The vowel does not correspond with that of the O. N. vb. *velja*, which should have become *well*. But the forms *dwall* from O. N. *dvelja*, and *hale*, O. N. *hella*, appear in Sco. *Wale* may be a formation analogous to *hale*.

Waith, *sb.* the spoil of the chase or of fishing. Wallace, I, 386. O. N. *væiðr*, a catch in hunting or fishing. Norse *veidd*, the chase, *veida*, to hunt. On Sco. *faid*, a company of hunters. See I, § 22.

Wandreth, *sb.* sorrow, trouble. Douglas, I, 88, 14. O. N. *vandræði*, difficulty, trouble. Norse, *vanraad*, misery, poverty.

Want, vant, *vb.* lack, stand in need of, suffer. Montg., S., 48, 3; Lyndsay, 152, 40704; Bruce, V, 422; Burns, 113, 2, 3. O. N. *vanta*, to lack. Norse *vanta*, lack, never means desire. This is the regular use of the word in Sco.

Wanthreivin, *adj.* unthriven, miserable. Montg., F., 327. O. N. *van* + *þrifenn*, Norse *vantreven*, O. N. vb. *þrifa*, Norse *triva*, *vantriva* (refl.). See Skeat under Eng. *thrive* and *thrift*.

Wap (wăp), *vb.* to turn, overturn, throw, hurl. Douglas, I, 2, 20; III, 167, 28; Gol. and Gaw., 127. O. N. *vappa*, to waddle. Norse *vappa*, turn, wrap around. Sw. dial. *vappla*, wrap up. Cu. *wap*, to wrap.

Ware, *vb.* to lay out money, spend. Rolland, III, 450; Dunbar, 92, 13; R.R., 3553. O. N. *verja*, to invest money. See Wall.

Waur, *vb.* to overcome. Burns, 7, 1, 7; Psalms, CXL, 2. See *werr.* Cp. Eng. *worst* as a vb. and superlative of bad, worse.

Weik, *vb.* to weaken. Scott, 68, 14. Cp. Norse *veikja*, to weaken, make weak. O. N. *væikja*, to grow weak, both from adj. *væikr*, weak, same as O. E. *wâc*. The Sco. vb. may be formed directly from the adj., in which case its origin becomes uncertain. Skeat says Eng. *weak*, M. E. *weyke* (which replaced *wook* < O. E. *wâc*), is from O. N. *væikr*. But the M. Sco. form of O. E. or O. Nhb. *wâc* was *wâke* (wçk); our word could come from this. The diphthong, however, rather indicates that it comes from the Norse vb.

Weill-varandly, *adv.* in a proper manner. R.R., 911. See *farrand.* Cp. O. N. *fara vel*, Norse *fara vel*, to go well, *velfaren*, gone well.

Welter, *vb.* to roll, turn, overturn. Bruce, XI, 25; III, 700; Douglas, II, 125, 25; T.M.W., 439; Lyndsay, 342, 770. O. N. *valtra*, to be unsteady, not firm, easily shaken. O. Sw. *valltra*, Sw. dial. *välltra*, to roll.

Werr, were, war, var, waur, *adj.* worse. C.S., 57; Lyndsay, 428, 1392; R.R., 589, etc. O. N. *verr*, worse, Norse *verr*, *verre*, Dan. *værre*, Sw. *värr*, Cu. *waar.* This is the modern Sco. pronunciation of it. The O. Fr. *wirra* does not correspond to the Sco. forms of the word. It is most common in Scotland and N.W. England.

Wicht, *adj.* strong, vigorous, skillful. Bruce, VII, 263; Ramsay, I 253. O. N. *vígr*, fit for battle, skilled in war, from *víg*, battle, Sw. *vig*, active, M. E. *wiht*, valiant. B-S. queries the word, but thinks it may come from M. L. G. *wicht*, heavy, thus the same word as Eng. *weight.* This meaning is, however, not satisfactory. The Sco. usage is that of the Scand. word. The *t* is inflectional. Cp. O. N. *eiga vígt um.*

Wick, *vb.* to make to turn, to strike off on the side, strike a stone in an oblique direction, a term in curling, to hit the corner (Wagner). O. N. *víkja*, to turn, to veer, Sw. dial. *vik*, Sw. *wika*, Norse *vikja*, *vika*, to turn (causative). Dan. *vige* not quite the same word.

Wilkatt, *sb.* a wild cat, Dalr., I, 723. Ramsay II, 500. O. N. *vill* + Eng., Norse *cat*, *kat*.

Will, vill, *adj. adv.* lost, bewildered, astray. Dunbar, 228, 74; Douglas, II, 24, 6, "to go will." O. N. *villr*, bewildered, *fara villt*, get lost, Norse *vill*, astray, Dan. *vild*, Sw. *vill*. Cp. Cu. *wills*, doubts, "Aaz i' wills whether to gang or nit."

Wilrone, *sb.* a wild boar. Scott, 71, 106. O. N. *vill*, wild, + *runi*, a boar, a wild boar, Norse *rone*, *raane*, Sw. dial. *råne*, Dan., with metathesis, *orne*.

Wilsum, *adj.* errant, wandering. Douglas, II, 65, 16; "a wilsome way," "Freires of Berwick," 410. See *will*, astray. *Wilsum* more frequently means "willful," is Eng.

Wissle, vissil, wyssil. Douglas, III, 225, 8; Bruce, XII, 580; Montg., F., 578. O. N. *vixla*, to cross, to put across, *vixlingr*, a changeling (Cl. and V.), Norse *veksla*, *vessla*, to exchange, Dan. *veksle*. Sco. and Norse both show the change of *ks* to *ss*. The Norse form *versla* shows later dissimilation of *ss* to *rs*. This is W. Norse.

Wittir, *sb.* a sign. Douglas, II, 231, 16. See *wittering*.

Wittering, vittering, *sb.* information, knowledge. Bruce, IV, 562; Douglas, II, 185, 27. O. N. *vitring*, revelation, from vb. *vitra*, to reveal. Norse *vitring*, information, M. E. *witering*, id.

Welter, *sb.* an overturning. Winyet, I, 49, 22. See the vb. *welter*.

PART III.

1. The Dialectal Provenience of Loanwords.

The general character of the Scand. loanwords in Sco. is Norse, not Dan. This is shown by (*a*) A number of words that either do not exist in Dan. or else have in Sco. a distinctively W. Scand. sense; (*b*) Words with a W. Scand. form.

a. The following words have in Sco. a W. Scand. meaning or are not found in Danish:

Airt, to urge. O. N. *erta*. Not a Dan. word.

Apert, boldly. O. N. *apr*. Not Dan.

Aweband, a rope for tying cattle. O. N. *háband*. Meaning distinctively W. Scand.

Bauch, awkward. Not E.Scand.

Bein, liberal. Meaning is W. Scand.

Brod, to incite. O. N. *brodda*, id. Dan. *brodde*, means "to equip with points."

Bysning, monstrous. O. N. *bysna*. Not E. Scand.

Carpe, to converse. Not E.Scand.

Chowk, jawbone. Rather W. Scand. than E. Scand.

Chyngill, gravel. A Norse word.

Dapill, gray. A W. Scand. word.

Dyrdum, uproar. W. Scand. The word is also found in Gael. Furthermore the form is more W. Scand. than Dan. Cp. *dýr* and *dør*.

Dowless, worthless. *Duglauss* a W. Scand. word.

Duds, clothes. Not found in Dan. or Sw.

Ettle, aim at. W. Scand. meaning. O. Dan. *ætlæ* meant "ponde over."

Farrand, handsome. This meaning is Icelandic and Norse.

Fell, mountain. W. Scand. more than E. Scand.

Gane, be suitable. O. N. *gegna*. Vb. not found in Dan.

Gyll, a ravine. O. N. *gil*. Is W. Scand.

Heid, brightness. O. N. *hærð*. Icel. and Norse.

Hoolie, slow. O. N. *hógligr*. Not in Dan. or Sw.

Kendill, to kindle. Ormulum *kinndlenn* is from O. Ic. *kendill* (Brate).

Lirk, to crease. I have not found the word in E.Scand.

Melder, flour. O. N. *meldr*. Is W. Scand., particularly Norse.

Pocknet, a fishnet. O. N. *pôki-net*. Not Dan.

Ramstam, indiscreet, boisterous. Both elements are W. Scand.

Scarth, cormorant. W. Scand.

Tarn, a lake. Distinctively Norse.

Tyne, to lose. O. N. *týna*. Distinctively Norse.

Waith, booty. O. N. *væiðr*. Icel. and Søndmøre, Norway.

Ware, to spend. N. *verja*. W. Scand.

Wick, to cause to turn. O. N. *vikja*. Not Danish.

b. The following words are W. Scand. in form:

Bolax, hatchet. O. N. *bolöx*. The O. Dan. word has the vowel *u*, *bulöx*.

Bown, O. N. *búinn*, cp. *grouf* < *grúfu*; *bowk* < *búkr*; *stroup* < *strjúpr*; *dowless* < *duglauss*, etc. The O. Dan. word was *boin*. The form in Orm. is *bŭn*, a Norse loanword.

Busk, to prepare, has W. Scand. reflexive ending *sk*.

Buth, O. N. *búð*. The O. Dan., O. Sw. vowel was *o*, *boð* and *bodh*, so in modern Dan. diall. In Norse diall. it is *u*.

Cappit shows W. Scand. assimilation of *mp* < *pp*.

Clubbit shows W. Scand. assimilation of *mb* < *bb*.

Drucken exhibits W. Scand. assimilation of *nk > kk*. Cp. O. Dan. *dronkne*,
   drone, but N.Dan. *drukken*.

Harn corresponds better to O. N. *hjarni* than to umlauted Dan. *hjerne*,
   O. Sw. *hiärne*.

Ill, will. Both show assimilation of *ld* to *ll*. Cp. O. N. *illr, villr*, but Dan.
   ilde, vild.

Rund, roond, is rather the O. N. *rond* than Dan. *rand*.

Ser, seir corresponds better to O. N., O. Ic. *sér* than to O. Dan. *sær*.
   This change of *e* to *æ* in Dan. was, however, late, i.e., in the last
   part of the 10th Century. See Noreen P. G.^{2} I, 526.

Slak, O. N. *slakki*. Shows W. Scand. assimilation of *nk > kk*.

Stapp, O. N. *stappa*. Has W. Scand. assimilation of *mp > pp*. Cp. *cappit*.

Stert is O. N. *sterta*. Cp. Dan. *styrte*.

Wandreth is nearer to O. N. *vandrædi* than to O. Dan. **vandraþ* (Brate),
   from which N. Dan. *vanraad*.

   Monophthongization of *ou* to *o*, *ai* to *i* (*e*), *öy* to *ö* took place in O. Dan.
about 900. The Scand. loanwords in Eng., where the monophthong might
be expected to appear, nearly always have the diphthong, however, which
as we know was kept in W. Scand. Have such words been borrowed from
W. Scand. then, or were they borrowed from Dan. before the period of
monophthongation? Danish settlements began in the latter half of the
9th Century, but Dan. (and Norse) and Eng. did not merge immediately.
Scand. continued to be spoken throughout the next century down to
the beginning of the 11th Century (Noreen). Brate says the majority
of loanwords probably came in in the beginning of the 10th Century.
Wall points out that the Mercian and the Northumbrian Gospels of
the 1st part of the 10th Century show extremely small traces of Scand.
influence. It would seem, then, that the greater number of loanwords
came in after monophthongation had taken place in Dan. The following
dates for the appearance of loanwords in the Anglo-Saxon Chronicle

may be of interest. These are all taken from Egge's article, "Norse Words in the A-S. Chronicle."

Hold first appears in 905, then again in 911 and 921; *law* in the present sense is first used in 959; in 1002 is first found the word *grith*, peace, which at once became common; *lætan*, to think, is first found in 1005. In 1008 appears *sagth*; in 1011 *hustinge*; 1014 *utlagian*; 1048 the noun *utlah*; 1016 *feologan*; 1036, 1046, 1047, *lithmen*, sailors; *lith*, fleet, in 1012, 1066, 1068, 1069, 1071; in 1055 *sciplith*; in 1036, 1041, 1054, 1045, and 1071 *huscarl*; *hamule, hamle* 1039; *ha* 1040; *hasata*, rower, (O. N. *há-sæti*) in 1052; in 1048 *bunda* and *husbunda*; 1049 *nithing*; in the same year also the phrase *scylode of male*, paid off (O. N. *skilja af máli*); 1052, 1066 *butscarl*, boatsman, *hytte* in 1066, *wyrre* 1066. In 1072 for the first time appears *tacan*; in 1076 *hofding* and *brydlop*, etc.

We may conclude that the Scand. elements that had come into O. Eng. in the beginning of the 10th Century were not large. From the middle of the century they came in in large numbers, but the period of most extensive borrowing seems rather to be the last part of the 10th and the first half of the 11th Century. Wall suggests that the Dan. spoken by the Dan. settlers in England was of a more archaic kind than that spoken in Denmark—that this might in many cases account for the archaic character of the loanwords. We know that the settlements in central England were predominantly Dan. as opposed to Norse. The Scand. place-names as well as the character of the loanwords in the Ormulum indicate that. It is probable, then, that monophthongation took place later in the Dan. spoken in England than in that spoken in Denmark. The following is a list of some of these words found in Scotch. O. N. *æi*, Dan. *e*: *bayt*, to graze; *blaik*, to cleanse; *graip*, a fork; *grane*, a branch; *graith*, to prepare; *laike*, to play; *slaik*, to smoothen; *lairing*, gutter; the Yorkshire form *lyring* (Wall) seems to show an original monophthong. O. N. *öy*: *careing, smaik*. O. N. *ou*, Dan. *ö*: *blout*, bare; *douff*, dull; *gowk*, a fool; *haugh*, a knoll; *loup*, to run; *louse*, loose; *nout*, cattle; *rowt*, to roar; *rowst*, to cry out; *stowp*, a beaker; *stour*, a pole.

It will be seen from the above, leaving out of consideration the diphthong *ou* and *ai*, that the character of a large number of the loanwords is Norse. In a great many cases the E. and W. Scand. form of the word was the same. There are, however, a few words in Sco. that bear a Dan. stamp: *sprent*, *donk* and *slonk* exhibit E.Scand. non-assimilation of *nt* and *nk* to *tt* and *kk*. *Snib* corresponds to Dan. *snibbe*, cp. M. E. *snibben*. All these have the umlaut. Eng. *snub*, M. E. *snubben* and O. N. *snubba* have the unumlauted vowel. *Bud* agrees closer with Dan. *bud*, *budh*, than O. N. *boð*, Norse *bod*. *Thraive* (Dunbar) and *threave* (Ramsay) both indicate an original *a*-vowel, hence correspond better to Dan. *trave* than O. N. *þrefi*. To these may be added *bask*, *flegger* and *forjeskit*, which are not found in W. Scand.

2. (*a*) The Old Northern Vowels in the Loanwords.

The values given in the following tables are for Middle Scotch. The symbols used do not need explanation:

Short Vowels.

a.

O. N. *a* in originally close syllable > *æ*, written *a*: *anger*, *hansell*, *apert*, *ban*, *blabber*, *slak*, *cast*, *chaff*, *dash*, *dram*, *bang*, *fang*, *stang*, *lack*, etc.

O. N. *a* in originally close syllable before *r* remains *a*: *bark*, *carl*, *carp*, *farrand*, *garth*, *harth*, *scarth*, *swarf*, and *harsk* (O. Dan.).

O. N., O. Dan. *a* in close syllable > *é* in *blether*, *forjeskit*, *welter*.

    a in close syllable > *ę* (*ay*, *ai*) in *aynd*, *baittenin*.

    a in close syllable remains *a*, written *o* in *cog*.

O. N. *a* in originally open syllable regularly becomes *ę*, written *a*, *ai*, *ay*: *dasen*, *flake*, *maik*, *scait*, etc.

O. N. *a* + *g* > *ę* written *ai* in *braid*, *gane* (to profit).

    a + *g* > *aw* in *bawch*. In *mawch* *ð* fell out and *a* developed as *a* before *g*.

e.

O. N. *e* remains in *airt, bekk, bleck, cleck, cleg, egg* (to incite),
   *elding, esping, fleckerit, freckled, gedde, gengeld, kendell, melder, mensk, nevin,
   werr, spenn, stert, sker.*

O. Dan. *e* remains in *sprent.*

O. N. *e* becomes *i* in *lirk, kitling,* and before *ng* in *ding, flingin, hing,* and also
   in *skrip, styddy.*

O. N. *e* > *æ*, written *a,* in *dapill, clag.* Cp. *sprattle* in Burns.
   > *æ* before *r* in *ware.*
   > *a* before *r* in *karling.*

O. N. *e* > *i* in *neefe (nieve).*

O. N. *e* appears as *u* in *studdy.* See word list.

O. N. *e* (from older *æi*) > *ç* in *hailse.*
   e + *g* > *e* written *a, ai:* e.g., *haine, gane* (to suit).

i.

O. N. *i* generally remains *i: bing, grith, kist, link, lite, titling, wilrone,* frequently
   written *y: byng, chyngill, gyll,* etc.

O. N. *i* before *st* > *e: gestning, restit.*
   i > *î* in *ithand (ythand),* and *ei* in *eident.*

o.

O. N. *o* remains *o: boldin, bolle, brod, costlyk, loft, rock,* etc.

O. N. *o* + *g* > *ow* in *low.*

u.

O. N. *u* generally remains *u: bught, buller, clunk, cunnand, lucken, ugg, clubbit,
   drucken, skugg.* The sound of *u* in O. N., however, was approximately
   that of *oo* in "foot."

O. N. *u* > *ŭ* in *drook.*

110

y.

O. N. *y* always becomes *i*, written *i, y*: *big, birr, filly, flit, trig, wyndland, gylmyr.*
The O. N. *y* had approximately the value of Germ. *ü*.

æ.

O. N. *æ* > *e* in *ettle*.

ö

O. N. *ö* > *e* in *gleg, glegy*, appears as *u* in *slut*.
O. N. *ö*, *u-v*-umlaut of *a*, becomes *æ*, written *a*: *daggit, ragweed, tangle.*
O. N. *ö*, *u*-umlaut of *a* in originally open syllable, like open *a*, > *ç* in *spale*.
Hence *u*-umlaut does not appear in loanwords.

ja (ia).

O. N. *ja* > *a* in *assle-tooth, harn, starn.*
    > *e* in *sker* and *stern*.

jö (iö).

O. N. *jö* > *a* in *tarn*.
O. N. *jö* > *i* before *r* in *firth, gyrth (gjörth), gyrthin.*

Long Vowels.

â.

O. N. *â* regularly > *ç*, written *a, ai, ay, ae, ei* (?): *baith, blae, bray, braith, fra, frae, lait, craik, ra, saikless, spay*, etc.
O. N. *â* + *g* > *aw, awch, aigh, aich, awsome, law*, sb. *law*, adj. *lawch*, beside *laigh* and *laich* in N. Sco.
O. N. *â* + *l* > *ow* in *chowk* (O. N. *kjálki*).

ę̣.

O. N. ę̣ remains in *ser, seir*.

 ę̣ > **ǣ**, written *a*, in *fallow*.

O. N. ę̣ before *tt* > *i*, written *y*, in *tytt*. Cp. *titt* in W. Norse dial.

î.

O. N. *î* most frequently remains *î*, written *i, y*: *flyre, gryce, grise, myth, skrik, rive, ryfe, tithand*, etc.

O. N. *î* appears as *e* in *skrech*, probably pronounced *skrich*.

O. N. *î* > ę̣, written *ei*, in *quey, gleit, keik*.

O. N. *î* > *ĭ* in *scrip, wick*, and before original *xl* in *wissle* (*wyssyl*).

The corresponding word in Norse also has a short vowel, but changed to *e, veksl, vessla* (and *versla*).

ô.

O. N. *ô* > *ū̆*, written *o, oo, u, eu*: *crove, rove, unrufe, hoolie, hulie, lufe, ruse, roose, sleuth, tume*.

O. N. *ô* > *ou* in *clour*.

 ô > *oy* in *toym* (Bruce), exact sound uncertain.

 ô + *l* > *ow* in *bow*.

ū̆.

O. N. *ū̆* remains in *buth, grouf*.

O. N. *ū̆* generally > *ou, ow*: *boun, bowne, bowk, cow, cour*, etc.

 ū̆ > *ô* in *solande, stot*.

 ū̆ > *ŭ* in *busk*.

ȳ.

O. N. ȳ regularly > î, written *i, y*: *lythe, tyne, sit, skyrin, snite.* Cp. *y.*

O. N. ȳ appears as *ç* (*ei*) in *neiris*, exact sound not certain. Cp. ȳ before *st* > *ĭ* in *thrist* (O. N. *þrýsta*).

ǣ.

O. N. ǣ remains in *hething.*

  ǣ > *e* in *sait.*

  ǣ > *e, e,* in *rad, red, radness,* etc.

Diphthongs.

ai.

O. N. *ai* > *ç*, written *a, ai, ay, ei*: *bait, bein, bayt, blaik, dey, grane, graip, graith, heid, laif, lairet, lairing, lak, laiching, thwaite, waith, slaik, swage, raise, tha.*

O. N. *ai* > *i* in *nyte* (?).

O. N. *ai* is represented by *i* before *r* in *thir.* Cp. Cu. *thur.*

O. N. *ain* > *en* initially in *enkrely.*

öy.

O. N. *öy* > *ç*, written *e, ai*: *careing, dey, smaik.*

  öy > *e* in *yemsel* (*yhemsell*), may be a case of Dan. monophthongation.

ou, au.

O. N. *ou, au* is regularly *ou, ow* in Sco.: *blowt, douff, dowff, gowk, gowl, loup, louse, nowt, rout, rowste, soum.* Very frequently appears as *oi, oy*: e.g., *soym, doif, goilk, loip,* etc.

O. N. *ou* > *u* in *gukk*, vb. formed from *gowk* (?).

jo.

O. N. *jo* before *r* > *a* in *starn* (O. N. *stjorn*).

    jo > *ei* in *leister*. Appears as *i* in the N. Sco. word *shiel*.

ju.

O. N. *ju* > *ŭ* in *stroop*.

    ju > *i* in *skyle*.

(*b*) The Old Northern Consonants.

b.

O. N. *b* regularly remains *b*.

    Is lost after *m* in *gylmyr*.

    b > *p* initially *pirrye*.

d.

O. N. *d* regularly remains.

    Is lost after *n* in *hansell*.

    An epenthetic *d* appears after *n* in *solande, ythand*; after *l* in *boldin* and *rangeld*.

O. N. *ld* > *ll* in *caller*.

g.

O. N. *g* regularly remains *g* before guttural and palatal vowels alike.

    g > ʒ before a palatal vowel in *genʒeld, yhemsel*.

O. N. *g* disappears after *n* in *titlene*.

    g > *ch* in *bawch, lawch*.

    On O. N. *a* + *g*, *o* + *g*, *e* + *g*, see the vowels.

p.

O. N. *p* regularly remains *p*.

> *p* > *ph* finally in *sumph*.

t.

O. N. *t* regularly remains *t*.

> *t* > *tch* in *scratch*.
>
> Seems to have become *d* in *cadie* (O. N. *kátr*), but Dan. *kådh* may be the source.
>
> An epenthetic *t* after *n* appears in *eident*.

k.

O. N. *k* regularly remains *k*.

> *k* > *ch* finally in *screch*. Cp. also *laiching*.

O. N. *ks* (*x*) > *ss* in *assletooth*, *wissle*.

> On O. N. *sk*, see *s*.

v.

O. N. *v* regularly becomes *w*: *welter*, *witter*, *ware*, *werr*, *wicht*, etc.

O. N. *v* is represented by *v* in *vath*, *vittirly*, *vyndland*, all in Bruce.

> An epenthetic *v* appears after *o* (*u*) in *crove*, *rove*, *unrufe*.

ð, þ

O. N. *ð, þ* quite regularly > *th*: *baith*, *bletherb*, *raith*, *buith*, *degraith*, *firth*, *garth*, *graith*, *ithand*, *lythe*, *mythe*, *hething*, *harth*, *grith*, *gyrth*, *waith*, *vath*, *sleuth*, *tath*, *skaith*, *wandreth*, etc.

O. N. *ð* > *d* medially and finally in *eident*, *ydlanlie*, *heid*, *red*, *duds*, *stud*.

O. N. *ð* is lost in *mauch*.

115

O. N. *þ* initially remains in *thrist, thra, thraif, tha, thir, thwaite, wan-threvin.*
   þ > *t* in *tytt, tangle.*

f.

O. N. *f* initially always remains.
   Medially and finally *f* remains in *cloff, nefe, lufe, laif.*
   Medially and finally *f* > *v* in: *nieve, nevin, rive, lave, crave.*
O. N. *f* > *th* in *scarth* (O. N. *skarfr*).
   An epenthetic *f* appears in *unrufe* (*v?*).

s.

O. N. *s* regularly remains *s.*
   s > *ch* in *chyngill* (?).

sk.

O. N. *sk* = *sk* initially medially and finally: *skar, sker, skewit, skill, skugg,*
   skrech, skant, scait, scool, scratch, scarth, skait, skail, scud, scudler, script,
   skyle, skeigh, busk, bask (dry), *harsk, harskness, forjeskit, mensk*(?).
O. N. *sk* > *sh* finally in *dash* (?).
   sk > *sh* before a guttural vowel in *shacklet* (?), and *schore* (?).
O. N. *sk* before *i* (*i̇*) > *sh* in *shiel.* Cp. *skyle* above.
   sk > *s* finally in *mense.*

h.

O. N. *h* initially before vowels remains, except in *aweband.*
O. N. *h* initially before *r, l, n,* is lost: *rad, rangale, ruse, lack, loup, nieve,* etc.
O. N. *ht,* remains, is not assimilated to *tt,* e.g., *sacht, unsaucht.*
   An inorganic *h* initially appears in *hendir, hugsum.*

O. N. *hv* regularly > *qu, quh*: *quhelm, quey.*

    m, n, l, r.

O. N. *m* regularly remains.

    m before *t* > *n* in *skant, skantlin.*

O. N. *n* always remains, *nd* is not assimilated to *nn*. Cp. Cu. *winnle.*

O. N. *l* initially remains.

    Medially and finally generally remains.

O. N. *l* after *o* > *w*: *bowdyne, bowne, bow.*

    l very frequently takes the place of *w* medially: *golk, dolf.*

    An excrescent *l* appears in *gylmyr.*

O. N. *r* regularly remains.

    Disappears before *sk* in *bask*, undergoes metathesis in *gyrth.*

    Inflexional *r* remains in *caller.*

FOOTNOTES

1.　The publications of the Scottish Text Society and those of the Early English Text Society are given first. The others follow, as nearly as may be, in chronological order.
2.　Ellis's D 31 = N. W. Yorkshire, Cumberland, Westmoreland and N. Lancashire.

BIBLIOBAZAAR

The essential book market!

Did you know that you can get any of our titles in large print?

Did you know that we have an ever-growing collection of books in many languages?

Order online:
www.bibliobazaar.com

Find all of your favorite classic books!

Stay up to date with the latest government reports!

At BiblioBazaar, we aim to make knowledge more accessible by making thousands of titles available to you- *quickly and affordably*.

Contact us:
BiblioBazaar
PO Box 21206
Charleston, SC 29413

CPSIA information can be obtained at www.ICGtesting.com
Printed in the USA
LVOW09s1449181015

458752LV00020B/734/P